Rising *from*

the Holocaust

THE LIFE OF FANNY GOOSE

Fanny Goose
with Janet Fridman

BELIEVE BOOKS
Life Stories That Inspire
WASHINGTON, DC

Rising from the Holocaust
By Fanny Goose with Janet Fridman

ISBN: 0-9787428-4-2

Library of Congress Control Number: 2007935820

Cover design: *Jack Kotowicz, Washington, DC, VelocityDesignGroup.com*
Layout design: *Annie Kotowicz & Jen Anderson*
Editing: *Elizabeth Moll Stalcup, Ph.D. & Rebekah Young*
Research assistance: *Barry Wells & Dan Brock*
Photo scanning: *Andrew Schulz, www.images.on.ca*

Believe Books publishes the inspirational life stories of extraordinary people from around the world. Requests for information should be addressed to **Believe Books** at www.believebooks.com. **Believe Books** is a registered trade name of **Believe Books, LLC** of Washington, DC.

Printed in the United States of America

To my husband, Jerry, our two sons, Martin and Steven, our daughters-in-law Heather and Michelle, and our grandchildren, Danielle (and her husband Darryl), Michael, and Rebecca. I love you all and am very proud of you.
—Fanny Goose

To my multi-continental family—despite the distance you are all near to me.
—Janet Fridman.

ABOUT THE AUTHORS

FANNY GOOSE lives in London, Ontario, and is known affectionately as "The First Lady of Downtown". She and her husband, Jerry,
are Holocaust survivors. They have two sons, Martin and Steven,
and three grandchildren. Fanny's survival story has previously been
captured in Steven Spielberg's Holocaust video project called the
Survivors of the Shoah Visual History Foundation.

JANET FRIDMAN, originally of Sheffield, Yorkshire, resides in London, Ontario with her husband, Professor Emeritus Gerald Fridman, and their two cats. She is the author of numerous articles and
short stories and the libretti for several musicals with composer/
conductor Brian Jackson.

And the remnant that is escaped of the house of Judah shall again take root downward, and bear fruit upward.

—From the Tenakh, 2 Kings 19:30

CONTENTS

FOREWORD

It is fitting that Fanny Goose's uplifting book is titled *Rising From the Holocaust*. Those of us, who are privileged to know her, know that Fanny rises to each and every challenge. Her indomitable spirit, her courage and humor, and her expansive and loving nature set the tone for everyone around her. Ebullience describes Fanny Goose, as she bubbles to the surface with her trademark directness, charm, and energy.

People call her "Mama Goose" because she mothers those around her. She cares for everyone, and my family and I are fortunate to have been the beneficiaries of that love. Since the first day I entered the world of politics in 1975, I could always count on Mama for unwavering support and unflagging work—highly valued commodities in that fickle environment. Whether the polls were for us or against us made no difference to her. That is the nature of her loyalty.

The Goose family is highly respected and admired. With diligence, patience, and intelligence, Fanny and her husband Jerry built a fine reputation in their city's business community. At the same time, they raised two outstanding sons, Martin and Steven, and now preside over a large and loving family.

Fanny Goose has a bottomless pit of love to share with her family, her friends, her community, and her country. This has helped her to deal with the painful adversity that she writes about in this book. Her constant ability to embrace life fully has allowed her to move on, never forgetting, but never letting negative events cripple her.

This story will inspire all who read it.

THE HON. DAVID R. PETERSON, PC, QC

1

A Tree is Planted

When I look back to that long ago time before my world shattered, I can remember nothing but happiness. There must certainly have been some temporary unpleasantness in my life but my memories are only of a golden time. Even now, the smell of Coty's L'Aimant perfume—very rare these days—brings back to mind a picture of my mother.

I was born Fanie Steinbock in the town of Skalat in eastern Poland, a lovely place situated on a pond that formed where the Gnila River widened as it flowed south. Less than 10,000 people lived in Skalat when I was a girl, but it seemed larger as it was the county seat and home to the courts, administration, and military for the surrounding district. The skyline was dominated by the tall spire of the Roman Catholic Church, the silvery-blue dome of the Ukrainian Orthodox Church, as well as four stout yellow towers capped by peaked roofs of red—all that remained of a sixteenth century castle. We Jews were so numerous that we had two synagogues, places where our rich heritage and religion were kept alive.

It was a wonderful place to grow up, surrounded by family and friends. The town had a thriving economy and our family was very comfortably situated. Although we lived in the town, my father and grandfather owned land in a nearby village and we had a thresher, quite a modern machine back then, which we loaned to the surrounding farmers at harvest time. We had a very close, happy relationship with the people my father hired to work on our farm; to each he gave a section of land on which to grow their own crops.

Our family was highly respected, and although we were Jews, we mixed freely with everyone. I have absolutely no memories of any type of discrimination or resentment, quite amazing since our little corner of Poland, *Galicia*, had been part of Austria up until World War I and was populated by Poles, Ukrainians, and Jews. Poland had a endured a stormy history since the mid 1700's, characterized by brief periods of independence and long periods of domination by Russia, Germany, and Austria. I was born just two years after the Treaty of Versailles granted Poland independence yet again.

When I was born, my father was out of town on business. My mother had sent word to him of my safe birth, but in her excitement she forgot to tell him the new baby was a girl. My father presumed somehow that I was a boy, and he made all the arrangements for the ritual circumcision before discovering the truth. Instead of having a *bris*, he decided to commemorate the occasion by planting a tree in the yard outside our house.

I went to the local public school, but also had a governess at home, Miss Sprenca, who taught me languages, and supposedly ladylike manners. The languages were her easier task! My grandfather Steinbock, a learned and devout Jew, presided over my religious education, teaching me Hebrew and Jewish history and instilling in me a strong respect for Judaism and for other religions. He was a close friend of the local priest and they had many theological and political discussions.

My sister Pearl was nine years older than I, and the beauty of the family. I remember her as glamorous and exciting. She was the local "belle"—blonde and blue-eyed. There was not a young man in Skalat—and quite a way further—who did not sigh after the beautiful Miss Steinbock. I found this much to my advantage, as I received many rides on motorbikes (forbidden but wildly exciting) and all sorts of goodies in exchange for "putting in a good word."

I was a tomboy who loved to play soccer with the boys. I was tiny so they did not expect much from me, but I delighted in giving the ball a hard, well-aimed kick and laughed when it clobbered them before they could see what was coming. I think they were a little afraid of me! I developed a very independent spirit which was at times to the despair of my mother and Miss Sprenca, but which on the whole they encouraged. I dressed as simply as I could, preferring my school uniform (pleated navy blue skirts and white blouses) to the frilly dresses worn by my sister Pearl.

In spite of the fact that I was not a boy as my father had expected, he was very good to me and often took me with him to social and business gatherings, making me feel that he really liked me. My mother owned a general store across the street from our home and was so occupied running the store—and discussing politics with the customers—that much of my upbringing was left to my paternal grandparents, Esther and Wolf Steinbock. Grandmother Steinbock oversaw our large white house and lived with Grandfather in the front of the house, while my sister and I, and our parents, lived in the back.

Grandfather Wolf had fled Russia while still a young man because of the increasingly virulent and frequent *pogroms* against Jews. His first stop was Skalat where he attended the synagogue and was immediately noticed. My great grandfather stepped forward to invite the well-educated, courteous young man home to *Shabbat* luncheon with his family. Wolf conversed freely with the family but he was particularly drawn to Esther, the Steinbock's beautiful and well-educated daughter. Although it was fairly common for young ladies to speak several Baltic languages, Esther also spoke French, quite a rarity back then.

The two young people found themselves attracted to each other and before long, plans were being made for them to marry. Wolf was happy to join the family business and to remain in Skalat. He dropped his Russian surname, so difficult for Polish tongues to pronounce, and took his bride's last name. After the marriage Wolf began an exporting business, which added to the Steinbock's already extensive holdings in land and livestock and expanded into a very thriving concern. Wolf and Esther had three children—two girls and a boy, my father, who they named Solomon.

Solomon was a nice, respectful boy, who was often seen offering to help widows in carrying their packages or with errands. He also willingly helped out in his father's business or his mother's store. As the only son in the family, his parents were protective of him. Grandfather Steinbock talked with the other businessmen of the community as his son grew to determine which young lady would be the best match for his handsome son—Solomon was tall with brown hair, a cleanly shaven face, and a quick smile. The family wanted a nice girl for their son to marry, but they also wanted a good economic partnership.

Ettie Greenberg was proposed as a good match for Solomon— she was attractive, intelligent, and well spoken. She came from a good family and would bring to the marriage her inheritance from her late father. She would have to agree, however, to live in Skalat, instead of near Podwolczyska, where she was living with her mother and step-father. Plans were set in place and my mother and father— Ettie and Solomon—were married in a traditional Jewish ceremony.

Ettie's mother—my maternal grandmother—lived in a castle, Zadniesowka, on the outskirts of Podwolczyska, a village about 32 miles west of Skalat, right on the Russian border. As a schoolgirl my heart had swelled with pride one day when my teacher read about the castle in *Ogniem Mechen*, a Polish history book by Henry Kenkecz and I had proudly called out, "That's my grandmother's castle!" In truth it was her husband's castle. My grandmother's first husband and my mother's father, Grandfather Greenberg, was a wealthy banker who had died young, leaving my grandmother with three small children. My young grandmother had then married a Mr. Summerstein, and with the new husband came a castle, which they converted into a hotel and restaurant. My parents often sent me there so I could get acquainted with my grandmother, who was reputed to be a great beauty, but I was too young to appreciate this. Although she gave me thick slices of bread piled high with home-made jam, and I enjoyed working with her in the garden, after two days I would tearfully beg to go home. I longed to be in the coun-tryside, on our own land a few miles outside Skalat, playing with my friends, the children of the farmers who worked our fields.

In 1935, two years after Hitler came to power, we began to hear rumors about the treatment of Jews in other parts of Europe. Some of these rumors said terrible things were happening in our own capital, Warsaw, but I was only thirteen, so I never gave it much thought. Even as the reports grew more menacing, there was a sense of disbelief. The Germans were a sophisticated, intellec-tual people, not like the Russian communists just thirty miles east, across the border. The Russians would seize a man's possessions and turn him out of his home. Surely Hitler could not be as bad as all that!

News traveled more slowly back then and we lived somewhat isolated from the cares of the rest of the world in Skalat. The year I turned fourteen, however, I remember sensing that my grandfather was worried although he never mentioned it to me. I often noticed him sitting and talking with the other men in anxious voices. Yet the rousing speeches I heard on the radio and the promises of a brilliant future for Poland were extremely optimistic. A new life appeared to beckon, and to clever, confident, independent Fanie, it seemed that my horizons were expanding and I had everything to gain.

In 1937, I turned fifteen and began a course in business studies at the local academy. I thoroughly enjoyed my studies, and when I enjoyed things I did well, so soon I was the prize student. By 1938 most people believed that war was inevitable—although this meant very little to me—my life was serene as always. My grandfather Summerstein thought it would be best to send my sister Pearl to relatives in the United States. His cousin, Dr. Emil Summerstein, was taking his wife to America—ostensibly to see the World's Fair in New York—and Pearl could travel with them.

Dr. Summerstein was a deputy in the Polish Parliament who was famous for his rebuttal to another deputy's anti-Semitic remark. The anti-Semite had said that Jews were not welcome in his political party because they "smelt of garlic and onions." Dr. Summerstein countered by saying that "Jews were indeed like onions—Jew haters peeled off layer after layer with their hatred, but these actions only brought tears to those who did the peeling!"

Anti-Semitism was on the rise—of that Dr. Summerstein was certain. He told my mother, "Hitler is coming to power and it will not be good for the Jewish people." From his privileged position in government he knew that many in power were Nazi sympathizers. The western part of Poland had been part of Germany prior to World War I, so many of the people who lived there had German roots. We called them *Pole-Deutsch*, or "Polish Germans," because of their divided loyalties. Of course, once Hitler invaded Poland, they dropped all pretenses and declared, "We are German!"

Dr. Sommerstein was able to get an exit visa for Pearl even though it had already become very difficult for Jews to obtain one. Although I was unaware of it at the time, my parents had discussed thoroughly whether I should also go, and decided that I was too young for such a radical step. Although it was kept quiet at the time, Dr. Sommerstein and his wife did not plan to ever come back to Poland, but Pearl was young and we assumed she would return. She never did.

The three of them sailed from Gdansk, Poland on August 15, 1939 on the ship *Batory*—as it turned out, the last ship to leave Poland. A week later, on August 23, Germany and Russia signed a non-aggression pact which secretly gave eastern Poland to the Russians and western Poland to the Germans, but this was kept from the people. On August 27, the Germans demanded that Poland hand over the port city from which my sister had set sail just twelve days before. The Germans renamed the port "Danzig", and five days later, on September 1, over one and a half million German soldiers marched east into Poland.

Britain and France had threatened to declare war if Germany invaded Poland and three days later, on September third, they did so. To me, all of this still seemed very far away since our little town was at the opposite end of the country, far away from the invasion, and as yet still untouched.

2

Life Under the Russians

The first shock that impacted us came on September 17th when hundreds of thousands of Russian soldiers marched into eastern Poland, singing as they came. They swarmed over our land—encountering no resistance—and in just two days marched west to meet the German army in the middle of Poland. Up to the moment the Russians crossed the border, we had assumed that the pact between Russia and Germany would not affect our lives. Now, just thirty miles from the Russian border, we were among the first to experience the new reality. We hoped Britain and France would intervene as promised, but ten days later, on September 27, Poland surrendered.

Soon there were Russians on every street corner proclaiming the wonders of communism. Even though we were very close to the border, we had not seen Russians before. The border was always closed, and visiting permits were very hard to obtain—even for those, like my grandfather, who had relatives on the other side. We had heard rumors about Stalin's tyrannical regime under which non-communists were persecuted and Jews were regarded with great disfavor. Now that the Russians controlled our town we had no idea of what to expect.

Even though the Russians claimed that life under communism was a utopia, we realized at once that the comforts we took for granted were incredible to them. They had never seen the variety and quantity of foods that we enjoyed, and they coveted it all. Within a week there were long lines for food as the Russians had confiscated all stores and businesses and handed them over to their own, usually incompetent, administration.

My grandmother owned a food warehouse that was an immediate target. She had sacks of flour, potatoes, and kasha—for making cooked grains—set aside in bags for the winter. Russian soldiers knocked on the front door of our house and demanded that my grandmother hand over the keys to her warehouse. She gave them the keys, then immediately took to her bed. Her sudden illness frightened me, so I crept next door to the home of a large family with many children, where the clamor of many voices singing and talking distracted me from my fears. When my grandmother died of a heart attack two days later, my family sent for me but I arrived too late to do anything but mourn her loss. My mother's grocery and convenience store was also seized; soon everyone began hoarding food and panic began to set in.

My grandfather was one of the first to be arrested. As a landowner he was labeled "bourgeoisie" and as such, considered an enemy of the communist state. They planned to send him to Siberia, but a large number of the townspeople presented a petition to the Russians asking for his release, as our family was very well loved in Skalat. They were endangering their own lives by protesting, but fortunately the Russians relented, and he was released. However, to demonstrate their authority they sent a group of soldiers to our home, demanding the cellar keys and confiscating anything they found. Our white stucco home with the long verandah across the front, the house in which we had always lived, was taken from us and we were forced to move into a much smaller one. I was still in shock from my grandmother's death, and horrified at this move, but I tried to be brave and accept what we were told—that our house was required by the "administration"—and determined to look instead to the future.

Meanwhile there had been no word from my sister, Pearl, and with the war rapidly expanding in our little corner of the world, my mother began to fear the worst. She would often cry for my sister, giving voice to fears that Pearl's ship had gone down at sea or been captured by the Germans. Possibly she was remembering the *Lusitania*, an ocean liner sunk by a German U-boat during World War I while on its way from the U.S. to Britain. I thought that my sister was probably safer than we were, but when I tried to say this to my mother she replied that she knew we were alive—we were standing right in front of her! My sister was somewhere unknown, perhaps on a boat in the middle of the ocean with the world at war. U.S. mail that reached our borders was not delivered because the U.S. was labeled a capitalist country and under communism therefore our "enemy." The Russians did not want anyone under their domain to learn about life in the U.S., so we could not even inquire as to the fate of the *Batory* without arousing suspicion. It was better to suffer in silence than to let them know that members of our family were on their way to the U.S.

The Russians mobilized all the young people. Boys were forced into the military and girls were assigned to other, often heavy, work. *How could I manage heavy work?* I thought, trying to come up with a scheme to avoid it. I had some training in bookkeeping from my time at the business school, and although I had not graduated, I also spoke a little Russian. *What about the bank?* Russia had seized all the banks, but they still had Polish customers so they needed employees who could speak both languages.

I went to the bank on a Saturday but as I looked around, I realized with a sinking heart that everyone in the place was of a lower class than the position in society my family had occupied just a few weeks before. Our social order had been turned on its head and my former place of privilege now worked against me. As soon as I gave my name they knew I was "bourgeoisie" and I was told, "We don't need any help now. We will let you know if we do." There was no use pretending to be poor when I applied for a job. Everyone in town knew my family.

Since I had no other job, the local government assigned me to the railroad crew where I was supposed to check the lines for damage and repair any breaks I found. Even though refusing was terribly dangerous, this assignment seemed ridiculous because I was barely five feet three inches tall and had no experience with this kind of work. I never even reported for duty. Looking back I see how very fortunate I was to get away with my insubordination because some of my friends, beautiful girls, were sent to Siberia for lesser infractions.

I decided to try again at the bank. This time I interviewed with the main bookkeeper, a Russian lady named Zarecky. As I sat opposite her, our eyes met and something passed between us, a recognition of sorts, and I knew at once that she was also from a privileged background. I felt her compassion and knew she would help me if she could. She went to the director, a fellow named Bolkowky, and explained that she felt I was the right person for the job. "She is young and willing to learn. I think she will be a great success. I know I can trust her." She did not say that I was from a good family—that would not have helped my situation—but I saw in Zarecky's eyes that look of satisfaction that comes from helping a kindred heart in need. I got the job.

"*Thank you, God,*" I whispered so no one could hear.

Life was much harder than we had ever known. There were long lines for food and fuel, and shortages of everything. Women would wear nightgowns on the street because they had nothing else to wear. The Polish winter was very harsh, and all of us who had been rich under Polish rule were now at the bottom of society. My family would have fared far worse had it not been for our friends, many former employees, who brought us bread, milk, and an occasional piece of meat. A number of farmers kept our livestock for us with the understanding that all would be returned when the Russians left.

My job at the bank was a great blessing. I worked diligently and enjoyed the work. Apparently my superiors approved of me, even though my nice dresses set me apart from my fellow employees. Once a week I was required to attend evening lectures where the teacher extolled the virtues of communism, but the lectures made little impact on me. It was obvious that what they were saying did not match reality. If life was so good under communism, why was everything in such short supply? A government store would get a load of sugar and people would line up at four o'clock in the morning to get a five-pound parcel. By eleven all the sugar would be gone while the line still stretched out the door of the shop and down the street.

Everyone used the black market to buy the "unobtainable"— even the communists! We could not run the bank without supplies and my superiors soon learned that I could convince even the most skeptical and cautious black marketers to bring forth their hidden wares. This was no small feat as buying and selling on the black market could get you five years in prison—if you were caught.

I would take the train to Lemberg, the nearest big city, to buy office supplies for the bank. The shopkeepers in the government stores would say that they had no pens, ink, paper or pencils, which was obvious—the shelves were bare. But when I asked where I could go to obtain the needed items, the lady behind the counter would size up my tiny frame, as if she were wondering, *Is this petite young lady a government agent?* Apparently passing the test, she would then usher me into a back room where the requested supplies would suddenly materialize—for a price! The shop managers also trusted me—in spite of my youth—and soon the bank learned that I was more successful on these missions than anyone else at the bank. So train rides to Lemberg, with a pocket full of bank rubles, became more frequent. Sometimes I had to visit several shops to get the needed goods, but I always took the train back to Skalat clutching a precious package of all I had set out to find.

All stores, all banks, and all places of business were owned by the state, but everyone skirted the system. Some of it was quite informal. My mother would make jam and let the neighbors know she had extra jars and soon the neighbors would come bringing white flour or sugar and they would trade. Occasionally a few rubles would change hands, but not often. This was illegal, as everything was supposed to be sold through official channels. In reality, even top communist officials would set aside part of every shipment to sell privately on the black market so they could pocket the money. It would have been impossible to function otherwise as the government stores had very little to sell.

I soon saw that despite the communists' altruistic claims, money was just as important in a communist government as it was everywhere else. Even though banks were under government control, they still had to function, which meant that they had to employ people who were efficient and pay them a decent salary—enough to make the employees value their jobs and remain honest. The names of all government employees, like myself, were put on a list and we became the only people in town who could go to restaurants. I could not take my own parents with me, but I could eat breakfast, lunch, and dinner in the restaurant, though I often chose to eat at home so I could be with my family. So as long as I had work in the bank, I was able to help my parents and live in reasonable comfort.

One of the worst things about living under this type of regime was that people were always being encouraged to inform against their neighbors in order to gain favor with the KGB—the Russian secret police. People would even make up stories if they thought it would gain them some advantage. Someone reported me as being friendly with the opposition, so the KGB came to the bank and arrested me. I was terrified.

They took me to the police station where they grilled me for several hours about my associates. They accused me of consorting with Polish officers and people of high society. I gulped. There was not a person in Skalat who did not know and love our Polish officers, and they often came to my mother's stores to buy goods and discuss politics. I did know them, but I was on no closer terms with them than with anyone in our small town. But I did not want to admit even knowing them to the KGB. I tried to persuade the Russians that they were talking about my sister, who had had many suitors among the handsome officer corps. "I am ten years younger than her," I insisted, "and was never part of that elite circle." Thankfully Pearl was beyond the reach of the KGB. And all of her powerful friends had fled when the Polish regime fell; they were now hiding in the forest or had already been arrested and shipped to Siberia.

I wondered if my parents knew where I was—news traveled fast in a small town—and later learned that a neighbor who worked with me at the bank had dropped by my home to tell my parents, "Fanie won't be home for lunch. She is being held at the police station." I am not sure what would have become of me, shipped to Siberia perhaps, had the bank manager and bookkeeper not come to the station to intercede for me. "She's a good worker," they insisted. "She is not anti-communist. We have not had any problems with her. She is honest. And we need her." After some intense and terrifying hours, I was released and allowed to go back to the bank.

Despite all the tensions and dangers, I was young and managed to have some sort of life. All the young men in our community had been mobilized into the Russian army, but there were dances on the weekends with Russian officers. My aim was to enjoy myself as much as possible under the circumstances.

3

The Horror Begins

In June, 1941 our bank manager, Mr. Bolkowky, announced that the Russo-German pact had fractured. "Germany and Russia are at war!" he said, looking around the bank as if to measure our reactions. Many of the girls my age were immediately inducted into the army, but since I was bourgeoisie and therefore of "impure" class I was exempted. The Russians made immediate plans to withdraw. We had to work feverishly closing accounts, under orders to pack bank records and the gold and jewels confiscated from the rich into boxes so it could all be shipped back to Russia. Needless to say, Mr. Bolkowky called it "a strategic retreat." No one would openly admit that the Germans were advancing. They simply said that they had to go back to Russia but would return soon.

My own uncle was conscripted into the Russian army and retreated with his unit into Russia where he was never heard from again. The bank wanted to take me with them to Russia as well. But when I told my Grandpa, he roared, "No, no, no! You are not going with them. When the Germans come all will be restored. They are good people. Everything will be better."

We had heard stories of what the Germans were doing to Poles, particularly Jews, but I, who had never experienced any form of persecution, could not picture those kinds of things happening *to us!* In spite of the bad times we were experiencing, life was still good, and I could not believe the horror stories. My parents and grandparents had experienced the horrors of *pogroms* years before and were very depressed, but even they told themselves that the stories must be exaggerated. After all, these terrors had happened under the barbarous Russians; the Germans were a civilized people!

The Russians left, and almost immediately the Germans jackbooted into town—no singing this time! We prayed for the best. A delegation of businessmen who had been prominent before the Russian invasion went out to welcome them. It was Saturday and the Jewish leaders wore their best *Shabbat* clothing, bearing flowers. All were pleased to see the Russians leave, because they hoped their businesses and land would be restored to them. To the shock and horror of all, the Gestapo officer in charge screamed out, "*Juden! Juden!*" and ordered the soldiers to open fire. We did not live far from the square—it was a small town—so we heard the shots. I ran to a neighbor's house, and hid with their large family. In the morning, my aunt—the very one whose husband had been conscripted into the Russian army—went to see what was going on and came home sobbing. About thirty men had been shot to death in the middle of the town, including my own dear Grandfather Steinbock. My heart broke. *How will I go on,* I thought, *now that both grandmother and grandfather are gone?* They were like parents to me. I was numb with grief and fear—it was all beyond comprehension.

The Germans immediately enlisted the help of the Ukrainian community, asking them to demand a *pogrom* against the Jews the next day. This was an excuse (not that the Nazis needed one) to get rid of the Jews by exploiting historical differences. The fiercely independent Ukrainians were under the fist of Stalin, and had taken Hitler's side because he had promised to free their land from Russian domination. Prior to that day Poles, Ukrainians and Jews had lived in peace together, but now even those with Jewish friends saw it as a way to appease the oppressors and save their own skins.

So the petition was signed and presented.

The next day, the Germans called out all Jewish men between 18 and 80 to report in the square for "work." They then asked the Ukrainians to find any Jews who were hiding and bring them to the square. They were immediately loaded onto trucks and driven away. All night we heard sporadic bursts of gunfire. The following morning the Nazis announced that 300 males, many younger than 18, had been executed at a defunct military base outside the city. The women were then allowed to fetch the bodies for burial.

The next night a *shivah* was held in one of the Jewish homes where we all went to mourn our dead. People were crying in a loud voice: "God listen to us! What is happening? What are you doing to us?" At first, even I, whose optimism had held up so far, was horrified and afraid. But somehow in the midst of that dark hour, something deep within me clung to the belief that God was a God of justice. I believed I would survive. My trust in God, instilled in me by my grandfather, solidified and I prayed that this nightmare would soon end. God surely had a purpose for my life and I was determined to fulfill it.

The Germans then announced that we must form a *Judenrat*—a representative group of Jews, as they did not want to deal with the Jewish community directly. This group would be responsible for enacting the orders of the Germans, and in exchange this group of Jews would receive "privileges." The *Judenrat* formed and we were all put to work. Because I had worked in a bank the *Judenrat* recommended me for a job as a payroll clerk at a road-engineering firm, Otto Heil. The company had taken up residence in Nowosiolka, because there was a large stone quarry there and the Germans needed stones to build the road they would use to invade Russia. Just three months after the Germans invaded our village, I found myself working for them.

All workers for Otto Heil had to live in a labor camp, Kamionki Number Three, which was run by the *Wehrmacht*, or traditional

German armed forces. This was not all bad because if you worked at Otto Heil, the SS, the army of the Nazi political party—whom we feared far more than the *Wehrmacht* because they were utterly wild—left you alone. There were about five hundred men in the camp, but only a handful of women, most of whom worked in the kitchen. Seven days a week we marched from the camp in Skalat to the work site in Nowosiolka, where the workers used dynamite to blast rocks in a stone quarry, and back again each evening, three to four miles each way.

The town was full of young soldiers, and although we all detested the Gestapo, there was one young, good-looking fellow named Hans who often watched me while I worked and occasionally stopped at my desk to talk. He seemed well mannered and I could tell he liked me, but he was in the SS and I was afraid to tell him that I was Jewish. One day he asked me to accompany him to a show in Skalat that weekend, and suddenly there was a huge knot in my throat. What should I do? Mixing with Jews was forbidden, but how could I tell him?

"I'm *Juden*. I am Jewish!" I managed to stammer, assuming that this would deter him, but he looked at me in astonishment and declared, "You can't be! Jews are ugly and dirty. And they smell! You are pretty. You are educated. You read books. You can't be Jewish!"

A week later, he stopped by my desk to say that he had written to his mother asking about me, "Mother, tell me the truth. I have met a pretty girl who is clean and well educated. She says she is Jewish. I am attracted to her and want to take her out. Is it true what they say about the Jews?" His mother had told him not to believe what he had heard about the Jews. "I have also met Jews who were very nice people," she replied. "But in a war it is best not to disagree openly with the powers that be."

His father was also in the army and a few weeks later his mother wrote to say that she had heard there were terrible things in store for the Polish Jews. If he wanted to save me, he must get me to Berlin where she had influence and could protect me. Even as he told me about her letter, the full horror of the situation did not penetrate. To me the thought of what my father would say if he heard of this little flirtation was far more frightening than anything a far-off Hitler might be planning. I was afraid of offending him, so I did not say yes or no.

Then Hans was sent to the Russian front, and two months later I received a letter from his mother telling me that he had been killed outside Stalingrad. She longed to see me and asked me to come to Germany, but I did not consider her offer. She asked me to send her a picture, but I did not respond. I could not imagine leaving my family, but I remembered her son fondly, so tall and handsome—and so naïve!

The *Judenrat* were ordered to resettle all the remaining Jews into a ghetto, and everyone, including those of us who were in the labor camp, were told to wear armbands identifying us as Jews. While the Russians had confiscated our large family home and moved us into a smaller home, now the German's forced my family into the poorest part of town where the houses were cobbled from whatever building materials the poor people who lived there could scrape together. The roofs leaked and our shrinking family—just my parents and my aunt—were crowded together with three other neighbors in a single small house. Occasionally I got permission to leave the labor camp after work and walk into town to see them, bringing food from the kitchen, but it always saddened me to see the hovel in which they now lived.

There were still approximately 3,000 Jews left in the area in and around Skalat—including some who had managed to escape into neighboring woods and others who had migrated into the area from surrounding regions. Even before the war, Polish identification documents had required Jews to state their "race," so it was easy to verify one's background. We had all lived in fear since the massacre, but it was not until early in 1942 that we heard that the *Judenrat* had orders for a "Final Solution." Jews were to be taken away, those over fifty first. The *Judenrat* knew the deportees were to be executed, so even they refused to do it. The Gestapo had to do it themselves.

It was while I was living at the camp that the Partisan forces hiding in the surrounding forest managed to break through the German line of defense and reach Skalat, forcing the Germans to withdraw. Poland had not formally surrendered to Germany and the home army continued to carry out raids, intelligence operations, and acts of sabotage against the Germans. My boss at Otto Heil, Herr Karl Hoffman, was German so he had to retreat with the Germans, but before leaving he entrusted his keys to me, and told me where the dynamite (used for blasting rocks) was stored. He knew the Partisans would be searching for it, and warned me that anyone suspected of collaboration with them would suffer terribly when the Germans returned—as was inevitable.

As soon as the Germans retreated, the Partisans came straight to the office and demanded the keys and the money from the safe. I had entrusted the cash to a close friend of mine, Wanda Czevchuk, who lived in a nearby village, telling her to guard it well and tell nobody, and I hid the most vital keys. I gave the Partisans the other keys, but of course they could not find the ones they wanted—the ones to a bunker where the dynamite was hidden.

Herr Hoffman was right. The uprising lasted less than forty-eight hours and the Germans were back with renewed strength, and the Partisans driven out. Immediately the *Wehrmacht* sent a car to the camp demanding Fanie Steinbock. My friends were terrified for me, and I too was very afraid. However, as soon as I returned the keys and the money intact, and they discovered the dynamite was untouched, I was allowed to go back to the camp. Later Herr Hoffman thanked me and said that we both would have been executed if the dynamite or the money had been touched.

4

Escaping the Genocide

One of my regular jobs at Otto Heil had been to go to the post office to send money the company earned, quarrying gravel, back to the company headquarters in Germany. One day I was there when my friend, Wanda, came in and whispered in my ear, "Fanie, I've heard from my friends with the police that the Gestapo is on their way from Tarnopol to interrogate you this very afternoon." I had done nothing wrong, but it did not matter. Undoubtedly someone had complained, "Why does a Jew have a good job that a Ukrainian or Polish girl could do?"

I was standing at the window mailing a package, but I turned to her and whispered, "Wanda, you've got to take my place!" I handed her the package and fled, leaving her standing in my stead. Just moments after I left, the Gestapo came into the post office and ordered her to come with them. They were from another town so they did not realize that they had the wrong young lady, but as soon as they got her to the local police station and began questioning her, some of the local officers asked, "Why are you questioning Wanda Czevchuk?"

"Wanda? This is Fanie Steinbock!" the Gestapo insisted.

"No," the policemen said, shaking their heads. "That is not Fanie, that is Wanda Czevchuk. We know her! We know her whole family. She is a good Polish girl!"

Of course all the officers knew Wanda because she was strikingly beautiful. The Gestapo looked silly and had to let her go. No one thought to ask how the mix up had occurred.

I had gotten away, but now where to hide? I dared not go back to the labor camp; the Gestapo would surely look for me there. I could not go to Wanda's home as they might be watching her now as well. My grandfather, as I mentioned earlier, had been a close friend of the priest in Krzywa, a village about a mile and a half to the east, where we owned our land. The Polish Catholic Church in Krzywa also owned land and before the war my father and grandfather used to loan their thresher to the church. Early in the war the priest had told my grandfather that Hitler wanted to kill all the Jews but my grandpa did not believe him. We thought that the Germans were good people, and we could not comprehend the horrors to come. The priest knew that he could not save our whole family, so he asked my grandpa to send someone—some member of our family whom he could hide, so our family would not be completely annihilated. My family had discussed sending me but I had not understood the severity of our situation and had not wanted to go. Now I remembered the priest's kind offer. It seemed my only hope, so I made my way to Krzywa, and told him what had happened.

He lived with his sister, who kept house for him, and the two of them hid me in their home for about six months. It was a good place to hide because the Germans left the priests alone for the most part at that point, but I could not go outside lest anyone recognize me and report my presence to the Gestapo. The sister tried to give me cooking lessons, but I had always been rather spoiled and I did not want to learn, so I ignored her and filled my empty hours with reading and crocheting.

At the end of 1942 the priest decided that I would be safer with his cousin in a monastery in Krynice. Before I went further from Skalat, I wanted to see my parents who were still in the ghetto; so that Saturday, the priest's sister took me to Skalat by night, and I snuck into the ghetto undetected. She was to come for me again on Monday morning. Once I was with my parents I had a wonderful welcome. Friends and all of my surviving relatives came to see me that Saturday. Everyone thought I looked well—after all, I had been protected, rested and fed for six months.

On Sunday I met some young girls who worked in the *Judenrat*. They told me they had been told to warn people that another *pogrom* was coming very soon. I went home to tell my parents, and they immediately began preparations. What food and clothes they had were put in the basement and in the attic in places they had previously arranged. My mother and aunt hid downstairs, my father hid in the attic of another house, and I hid in the attic of our house.

About three o'clock in the morning we were awakened from sleep by the sound of gunfire and people screaming. I looked out the attic window and saw Germans chasing people down the street. They were in a frenzy; dragging people out of their homes, beating them, and even killing them with their bare hands in full view of everyone. They machine-gunned down anyone who tried to escape in their wild orgy of killing. The killing spree continued until noon the next day, with the Germans going house to house, searching everywhere. I saw my aunt and my mother being led away by the Gestapo with the other neighbors. Then they found me and several other neighbors who were with me in the attic.

I was lined up with the other Jews in the street in a line so long I could not see the beginning or end. I felt quite numb, but still could not believe this was the end. Again I prayed to the God of my grandfather. "Please help me!" my heart cried out as I struggled to overcome my fears. I intended to do as I was told. They gave me some bread, and said that we were to be loaded onto a train—in cattle cars—for a long trip. We were told we were going to a "work camp" later to be known infamously as a concentration camp. I could not see my father, but my mother and aunt were nearby.

They were already loading the train when a young Italian soldier came up to me and offered me more bread, saying: "Take this, you will need it where you are going." My mother called to me," Don't take anything from him." As she was saying this, a young Jewish policeman from the *Judenrat*, someone I only knew slightly, came over to me and said loudly, "You can't go with them, you are my bride." He was trying to save me, as he knew quite well where we were going. He pulled me out of the line, and I screamed, "No, No! I want to go with my mother!" The Jewish policeman, who could have been killed if the Gestapo had realized what he was doing, grabbed my arm, shouting even louder, "You are my bride. Come with me." Then the Italian soldier came up, grabbed my other arm, and they both dragged me away. Looking back, I see the irony of the scene—I was hysterically crying to go with my mother to almost certain death, and here was an Italian soldier, an enemy, and a member of the *Judenrat* (a collaborator) risking their lives to save me.

They took me out of the ghetto. The policeman had to return to duty before he was missed, but he told me to run. The Italian offered to give me money, and also advised me to run and find hiding. *Where could I go?* I was outside the ghetto, and frantic about my mother's fate. *She might be on the train by now!* Suddenly a thought came to me. *Otto Heil where I used to work!* The Gestapo did not usually execute workers who had identity cards until their usefulness was over, and I might find someone there to help me. I had helped Herr Hoffman before, and he trusted me. He was a German, a civil engineer employed by Otto Heil, but certainly not a Nazi. I had heard him mutter under his breath things like, "Damned Hitler," and he was always upset when his workers were badly treated or worse, murdered by the Gestapo. Many times I had seen him make faces at the compulsory picture of Hitler or even throw it on the floor and say in a pained voice, "Enough is enough! You are damaging the human race!" when no one else was watching.

I went to see him and he was most alarmed. He knew I had left the city after the Gestapo had questioned Wanda, but he had no idea what had happened to me. He was fully aware of the deportation of the remaining Jews from our area. I told him that I had been hiding in Krzywa, but that I had come back to see my family and my mother had been taken away. "I want my mother," I cried, and he said he would do what he could. I knew this was hard for him because he always tried to avoid going out when the Germans were on a rampage, forcing Jews from the ghettos and onto the trains that went to the camps. The soldiers would work themselves into a mania, going after Jews with shocking intensity, almost as if they were temporarily insane. They not only committed atrocities themselves, but they also corralled innocent people into taking part, so Herr Hoffman always laid low when the SS were rounding up Jews. He was German but he hated what the Nazis had done to his country.

For my sake, he hopped on his motorcycle and zoomed off to the railway station, where he told the Gestapo bosses that he wanted Etta Steinbock as a laundress for the factory. They called, "Etta Steinbock!" and she was brought out of the train. For a brief moment he thought he would be able to save her, but the Germans took one look and said, "Oh no! She is too old. We'll give you a younger one." They forced my mother back onto the train and pulled off a younger woman.

When Herr Hoffman came back and told me what had transpired, he had tears in his eyes. "How could they tell me that she was too old?" he asked. I nodded mutely for my mother was only 42 years old.

5

Still Alive

The ghetto was now much smaller, and I hid with some friends for a few days. Then the priest from Krzywa came to the ghetto and, by clever questioning, found me. He sent me to the monastery he had spoken of before. It was now late December, and the priest in charge of the monastery was afraid I might give away the fact that I was Jewish, so he made me stay in my room much of the time. He insisted I wear dark clothing, the kind someone would wear if they were on a pilgrimage to a monastery, whenever I came out.

I was there for about six months, feeling very much alone in the world. My nerves were shaky and I walked the confines of my small room as if in a dream. I saw only a few people, the cleaning lady and the woman in charge of the kitchen, who brought me my food. I worried about my family, fearing the worst and hoping for the best. *Perhaps my mother and aunt had escaped and were even now back in the ghetto,* I thought wistfully. There was no way to know what was going on outside the walls of the monastery. I would look in the mirror and see a young, good-looking girl looking back at me and wonder, *Am I waiting to die? Will they get me?* My dark thoughts seemed overwhelming, but then an hour later they would vanish and I would feel more like my usual optimistic self.

It was difficult to sit idle in the monastery with only my fears for companions. I was completely isolated, with no news of Skalat, constantly wondering if by some miracle my mother might have escaped and returned. I had a dream in which my grandfather was reading the holy book, and said "Fanie, you must leave the monastery. You will be okay."

By August I felt that I had to get out of the monastery. I had to have some word about my family. In my dark pilgrim's habit I went to the outskirts of Tarnopol, a larger city some 20 miles west of Skalat where I saw a group of Jews—easily recognizable by their yellow armbands—working on the road. A German soldier and a Ukrainian policeman were guarding them. When I tried to get near enough to speak to them, they moved away obviously afraid that I might harm them. I managed to get a few words of Yiddish out without the guards hearing, and one woman heard me. "Don't worry I am Jewish, too," I explained. "I want to go with you." I followed them at a distance back to their work camp—the Janowska camp outside Lwow, Poland. I had to be very careful that the guards did not suspect I was following them.

I followed them into the *lager*, or work camp, and there was Mr. Zimmerman, the head of the local *Judenrat* from Skalat. He recognized me right away and was upset to see me there. He had been a friend of my family's before the war and was there that day because the camp also housed the Gestapo headquarters for the whole region. He was not under such strict supervision, and managed to get away to speak to me. "Why have you come here?" he wanted to know. "You were in a safe place!" He told me there was nothing left in Skalat; more Jews had been killed and sent away to the camps. Now that the Germans were losing the war they were clamping down even more rigidly. The labor camp in Nowosiolka was being shut down too, as there were no more roads being built. The Germans were retreating as the Russians advanced, reclaiming their previous territory. The German commanders made eliminating Jews a priority.

"The Germans are killing Jews right now in the ghetto," said Mr. Zimmerman. "Only last week 3000 Jews were killed by machine guns in the work camp at Janovska in one afternoon." He told me that he believed my father was still alive and in hiding with our family lawyer, Mr. Lempert and his family, somewhere nearby. He had no details, of course. All this made me more determined than ever to go back to Skalat. Mr. Zimmerman was furious. "It is your duty, Fanie to stay in the monastery and survive so someone will remain to tell the story of Skalat. Your father knows you are safely hidden and it is a great comfort to him."

"I can't go back!" I cried. "I have to have some word about my family. I have to see for myself."

"I can't keep you here. My work quota is already full and the Germans will demand an explanation if an extra girl suddenly appears!"

"If they kill me, they kill me," I declared. "I have nothing to lose. I have to go back."

We decided that I would return to Skalat with him on a bus, surrounded by Gentiles who had come to Tarnopol for the day, hoping that no one would recognize me in my hat and dark clothes.

6

"Judenfrei"

My old labor camp, Kamionki Number Three, was even more terrible than I remembered. Many people had died of disease or had been killed outright. The ghetto had been completely liquidated. The Otto Heil Company in Nowosiolka was still functioning, barely, and provided the only work in town besides the railway. The workers in Kamionki Number Three knew that soon the stone quarry would cease operation, the camp would close, and all the workers would be eliminated.

How terrible everyone looked. Yellow skinned and emaciated, they barely had the strength to continue. The few people of my own age looked as if they were 100. I was healthy and well fed, and they were all worried that I would be noticed and killed immediately. I again went to my trusted ally Herr Hoffman. He was amazed to see me, and thought I had been very foolish to jeopardize my safety, but he agreed to help me. He decided I should work in the kitchen because it was the least likely place anyone would look for me. So there I was—I had no idea how to cook, but again God was kind to me. An older woman in the kitchen, whose job was cleaning and washing up, was an excellent cook, so we traded jobs—she cooked and I cleaned. I was delighted to find that my old friend Wanda was still working for the company, and because she was not

Jewish she did not have the fear of being shot hanging over her. However there were still perils she had to face. She was very pretty and one day to my horror I overheard that she was in a group of girls singled out to be sent to Germany. Again, I appealed to Herr Hoffman, and this time he was able to save her, saying he needed another girl for the kitchen.

I stayed with Wanda and her mother and brother who showed immense courage in sheltering me. Her brother Bronak was involved in a clandestine butcher's business. Rationing was very strict, with all the best going to the Germans, but occasionally there was a chance to get an animal secretly from a local farmer and share it out among the locals.

One day they managed to get hold of a pig, which they butchered and then took to the Czevchuk house to be cured and shared with the others. However, the Germans became suspicious and sent a party of soldiers to search the house. Wanda and I were still sleeping so they put the pig (fortunately drained of blood) into our bed and tucked it well in under the covers. We were told to pretend to be asleep, and when the Germans opened the door and saw two young ladies lift their tousled heads, they apologized for waking us, closed the door and moved on.

We all hugged each other in our relief at our narrow escape, and were so pleased we had retained the pig. Then suddenly, the funny side struck us: in order to hide the pig, they had used me, the Jewish girl they were hiding—as a cover!! The penalties for concealing a Jew were much more severe than for hiding a pig, but the risk they were taking never seemed to have occurred to anyone. It seemed to be terribly funny, and we laughed a lot, a rare happening in those days. Then the seriousness of what we had done, and the awful chance we had taken sank in, and it did not seem so funny. But we had gotten away with it—pig and all.

The time for the closing of Otto Heil was drawing closer. Everyone was prepared for it, and all were very depressed. As there was no more work, we were no longer useful, and we all knew that meant liquidation. One night there was a huge party in the camp. Many people were there, German and Ukrainian soldiers, senior officials from the railroad and all of the workers. Everyone was drinking and having a good time.

The chief railroad official, someone I had known since before the war, suddenly came up to me and said, "Okay Fanie, it is time to go."

I leaned back and looked up at him. "Why should I go?" I asked. He said nothing.

"You are scaring me," I said. "Why should I leave?"

He leaned forward and whispered into my ear. "They are going to start killing Jews soon. Everyone is going to be liquidated tonight."

I stood up, took his arm and walked out the door. As we left he told the guards that I was his secretary. As I still looked reasonably healthy compared to the other workers, they believed him and we were allowed to leave.

We were no more than fifty feet from the building when we heard the ratta-tat-tat of machine gunfire.

The party was celebrating the fact that Skalat was to become *Judenfrei* or "free of Jews" that very night. The remaining 73 women and about 40 men lay dying, within minutes of our departure.

The official who had saved me told me that I could hide "for that night only" in an attic at the railway station. "Tonight they will be too drunk to care about anything," he said, "but tomorrow they will hunt down any Jews who have escaped. You must get away from here as soon as possible."

He was right of course, and I immediately realized I could not go back to the Czevchuks. They were too near, and there was always the chance that some soldier might recall Mrs. Czevchuk's "niece" and go back to check on her. From my corner of the attic I could hear drunken revelry all night, interspersed with cries of "*Judenfrei*" and bursts of raucous laughter. I shook with fright and wondered if I was the only Jew in Skalat left alive. Part of me was proud that I had evaded the Nazi killing machine, and I muttered to myself "Not quite *Judenfrei*." But most of the time I was racked with fear and trying to think of where to go next.

Then an idea came to me. Mr. Bohannic, a farmer who had worked for us as the overseer on our land, had a small farm of his own in Krzywa. This was about five miles from Skalat. *Could I find my way in the dark?* Mr. Bohannic had been a close friend of my father, and had been involved in local politics before the war. He was a man I could trust. He had even hidden some of our cows on his own farm, promising to return them after the war. I knew too, that even though the Germans had forced him to work on the railroad, back in 1942 he had managed to smuggle bread into the ghetto to help us. I would see if he would help.

7

The Loyalty of Friends

I left before it was light, and made my way to the Bohannic farm without incident and carefully climbed up the side of their house and into the attic above their home, keeping as quiet as possible. I did not want to show myself immediately, as there was also Mrs. Bohannic and their son and daughter, and any one of them could have turned me in. The attic extended over a breezeway where they kept a few chickens below.

I had been good friends with the Bohannic daughter, Bronnia, before the war as we were about the same age and we had often played together during harvest time. It had not mattered that I was the owner's daughter and she was the daughter of one of my father's workers; we were dear friends. I hid there for a couple of days, living on dried bread, which they had stored in case there were food shortages, some vodka, and dried garlic, all hidden in the attic as well as raw hen's eggs that I gathered in the early morning before the family was up.

One day I heard Bronnia below me, gathering eggs, so I called out softly, "Bronnia, Bronnia, I am here."

"Oh!" she said, "where are you?"

As she came into view, she made the sign of the cross as if she was not sure if I was a ghost! "Fanie, it is you!" She exclaimed.

"How did you get here?"

"Shssh!" I whispered. "Don't say anything! Just tell your father that I am here and ask him if he wants me to leave."

"Oh!" Bronnia cried, "my father will tell you to stay! The war is not going well for the Germans and will soon be over."

Later Mr. Bohannic came up to the attic and insisted that I stay. He urged me to show the utmost care lest I betray them all. Only his wife and daughter must know I was there. He felt that protecting me was his own contribution against the Nazis. He was a fierce Polish nationalist, and told me that he was very worried about what would happen next. As the Germans weakened their grip, tensions were already rising between the Poles and the Ukrainians. Both nationalities had terrorist groups and both groups were already making guerrilla strikes and murdering each other. The Germans, of course, encouraged this as it did their job for them.

I pondered all this as I hid in the barn. *What sort of world was this in which so many factions wanted to kill each other? Why would the Germans spend so much time exterminating Jews when they could use the time and energy to defend their homeland before they were totally defeated?* I heard afterwards that in Warsaw, Hitler had ordered that precious reserves of fuel be used to blow up as much of the city as possible. Apparently he had said, "Warsaw is the heart of the Poles, so I must destroy the heart." Again I heard my Grandfather Steinbock's voice, "We shall survive, little Fanie. Many dictators have tried to destroy us, but we rose again. Now is the time for courage."

Mrs. Bohannic and Bronnia brought me food. To avoid suspicion, Mrs. Bohannic played the part of an avid anti-Semite. She would argue with the neighbors if they expressed any pity for what had happened to the Jews, and tell them that she had hated the fact that her husband had worked for a Jew. "The Jews stank," she would say. "The place is better without them." She would usually end her diatribe by saying how glad she was that our district was now *Judenfrei*.

I knew what she was doing, but it still unnerved me to hear her words when she spoke to the neighbors in the yard right below my hiding place. She was so convincing that I wondered at times if she meant it. But I knew that it could not be true, that she was only saying such terrible things because she wanted to erase any trace of suspicion, as all the neighbors knew that her husband had been a good friend of my father's before the war.

Although German power was diminishing, the violence continued. One night at about 4 o'clock, I heard a disturbance in front of the house, and voices calling, "Bohannic, Bohannic, come out." Mr. Bohannic began to cry, and was pleading with them to go away. "What do you want with me," he called plaintively, "I have a wife and children and only want peace." The intruders were the Banderossi, the Ukrainian terrorist group. Mr. Bohannic pleaded with them for about two hours, and they finally threatened that if he didn't come out, they would burn down the house with them all inside. Eventually Mr. Bohannic came out. The sky was growing lighter, so I could see the whole thing from the window. They put a rope round Mr. Bohannic's neck and tied it to a horse. They then set the horse off at a gallop. Poor Mr. Bohannic was screaming as his body was dragged over the uneven ground as he strangled to death. It was horrible to watch such a grim scene. Once they were sure he was dead, they left, but it was not until noon that Mrs. Bohannic had the courage to go retrieve the body with her son.

The tragedy was not yet over. A few days later they held a funeral for Mr. Bohannic, and many neighbors attended. As the family was leaving the cemetery, the Banderossi reappeared, and shot the son in full view of everybody. This constituted a warning. Needless to say, very few of the neighbors dared attend the son's funeral.

I was worried that the murders might have something to do with hiding me, but Mrs. Bohannic said this was not the case. It was Mr. Bohannic's politics that the Ukrainians were punishing. He had been a well-known Polish nationalist, and although he had been very quiet, the Ukrainians knew he was well liked and trusted, and felt he might become a leader when the Germans were finally gone and the struggle between the Poles, Russians and Ukrainians took the stage.

For the first few days after these incidents, the Bohannics were overcome with grief, and often forgot to bring me food. I again survived on raw eggs, garlic, dried bread, and vodka, which had been stored in the attic for the winter. I felt that I was a terrible responsibility for them to shoulder, but when I haltingly mentioned it, Mrs. Bohannic, brave woman that she was, said that I should stay. "After all, Fanie, where else can you go? My husband took you under his protection, and it would be an insult to his memory if I betrayed his trust."

I survived like this for the next few months until March 1944, when we heard that the Russians were approaching rapidly. They were already across the Polish border, and would soon reach Krzywa. A Polish underground newspaper came into circulation, and for the first time we received detailed news about the progress of the war. The editors had access to Russian, Swiss and BBC broadcasts, so the news was up to date and reliable. We learned that the Germans had not been able to capture Stalingrad, at a terrible cost to both sides. Now the Russians had regained Kiev and the Allies were in control in North Africa and had landed in Italy. We recovered optimism. The war would soon be over.

Then the Germans made a public announcement, advising everyone to leave Krzywa, and withdraw to Zarbensky, a village about five kilometers away, as Krzywa was about to become the battleground for the confrontation between the Russian and German forces. To my joy I heard that Skalat, just two miles away, had already fallen to the Russians.

The remaining Bohannic family decided to take this advice and go with the rest of the villagers. Bronnia came to me and said they would willingly take me with them as part of their family, but I was nervous. I had been in hiding so long and was still afraid that someone might recognize me as a Jew and hand me over to the Germans. So I elected to stay and take my chances there. I was touched by the fact that despite their own tragedies, the Bohannic family was still prepared to support me. I think in some way they regarded me as a symbol of hope. For me they were angels of mercy. They were quite sad that I had decided to stay on without them, but left me well supplied with food and water.

The next day, Sunday, the battle started in earnest. It was fantastic and horrible. Most of the houses, including the one where I was staying, had straw roofs that would go up in flames very easily. There were bombs falling everywhere, and the loud percussion and fires went on for three days non-stop. I could not sleep; my ears were ringing with the incessant noise. One night the Germans took cover in the passageway below where I was hidden; they were there all night shooting and screaming orders. Bullets passed through the thatched roof of my shelter but by some miracle I was not hit and the roof did not catch fire.

In the midst of this terror, deprived of sleep and too frightened to eat or drink, I saw a vision of the Virgin Mary, coming for me holding out a blue robe. I heard her say, "You will be saved." She put the robe on me and carried me across a large body of water. It was a great comfort to me, as I believed it was a sign that God would protect me.

At last the world was still. An hour later we heard singing, *in Russian!* I recognized the song—it was the same one the Russian soldiers had been singing when they marched into Skalat five years before. I looked through the miraculously unbroken window—sure enough Poles and Russians were singing and dancing everywhere. The Russians were victorious! This was a tremendous relief because the Ukrainians had killed many Poles like Mr. Bohannic and now the Russians would stop them.

I was still too shaken to leave the house, but three days later the Bohannics returned and I heard them calling: "Fanie, Fanie. Are you all right?" They rushed up the stairs to see me and were amazed to find I was totally unhurt. They took me outside, and I realized why they were so surprised to find me untouched. Every house and structure in that part of Krzywa was destroyed. The sole exception was the Bohannic home.

Mrs. Bohannic insisted I have a hot bath. All the children fetched water and heated it; we then filled the old tub in the bathroom with hot water. I luxuriated in it—my first bath in eight months. It was wonderful and I shall never forget how I felt the tension leave me as I soaked. I felt reborn, and immediately announced my intention of going to Skalat. If I had been part of one miracle, who knew what others there could have been. Maybe friends, neighbors—perhaps even my own family—had survived as well.

Mrs. Bohannic took my hands gently, "I do not like to have to tell you this Fanie," she said quietly. "That is why I wanted you to feel calmer after a warm bath. But I have made inquiries, and both your parents have perished. Your mother was gassed at Treblinka shortly after she arrived. And your father and his group were killed in an accidental fire just a few days ago. The town of Skalat is gone—they are selling the bricks from the ruins." There had been rumors about the death camps circulating for some time, and as the Germans retreated, the Polish underground press had confirmed the reports. In my heart of hearts I had known my mother and aunt were dead long before Mrs. Bohannic stripped away any illusions of hope, but as far as I knew, my father was still alive. Now nothing remained.

It was too much for me. *I had to get to Skalat. Surely someone had survived and was looking for me!* My father's death seemed the most tragic because it seemed so unnecessary. He had managed to survive the entire war, hidden in a barn near Nowosiolka with our lawyer, Mr. Lambert and his wife, his mother-in-law, and her sister. When they heard that the Russians were near they celebrated with vodka and a single cigar, which set the whole place ablaze killing everyone. After successfully eluding the Nazis for two years, my father had perished just days before Russians drove out the Germans.

The Lamberts were survived only by their little daughter, whom my mother had helped to hide at the beginning of the Nazi occupation. At first we could not believe that Hitler would target Jewish children, but once that was clear, my mother had found a place to hide her with some Gentile friends in Zadniesowka, near where my mother had grown up. Now both mother and father were gone and the little Lambert girl was an orphan. After the war, her relatives in the U.S. found her through the Red Cross, and brought her to the States, but I do not know where she went and have never seen or heard of her again.

8

Return to Skalat

I had to go to Skalat. I had to know if somebody—anybody—from my old life had survived. *What else did I have?* Mrs. Bohannic was worried for my safety as I was young and pretty, and she had heard many stories about Russian soldiers raping women. She said I would have to be disguised as an old woman. She made me wear rags—not that my own clothing was much better, and dirtied my face and made it look wrinkled. Then she gave me a cane, and told me to limp convincingly.

We went to the highway and soon a Russian military truck—the only type of transport there was—stopped, and the soldiers helped me on, calling me *Babushka* or "old woman." I had fooled them so far.

We came to a sign that said "Skalat," so I asked the soldiers to stop, even though I could see nothing but ruins. I was so excited that I threw away my cane and jumped from the truck. Immediately I realized that Mrs. Bohannic had been wise, as the moment the Russians realized I was a young girl, they began calling after me, "Hey girl, come back. We want you!"—as well as various obscene suggestions. I ran like mad, and found that I was near the area in which Wanda Czevchuk's family lived. It was a strictly Polish area where no Jews had been allowed to live, so it was not so badly damaged. Wonder of wonders, the Czevchuk home was still standing, and they were there.

They were amazed and delighted to see me, and told me that the part of town where we had lived was totally destroyed. Wanda and her family welcomed me, and decided to give me a party to celebrate my escape, inviting family and close friends. They all went to church to thank God for my survival, but I remained home alone. There was no talk of my going with them, as it was still very dangerous for the few remaining Jews to be out in public because the populace had become so accustomed to attacking Jews at will—with no consequences. Tensions between Poles and Ukrainians, who had sided with the Nazis, were high and after witnessing the awful death of Mr. Bohannic, I was afraid of the Ukrainians in our town.

The only Jews who remained were those who had gone into hiding. Before the war, the Jewish people had made up almost a third of the population; yet only two percent had survived of the thousands who once filled our little corner of the world. Now those few survivors crept out of their hiding places.

I went to visit the site of our old house. The entire area was devastated, without a brick or stone to mark the place where the houses had once stood. I was struck dumb by the ache in my heart. *I had survived for this? To live alone? With nothing? No relatives? No loved ones?* As the tears rolled down my face I noticed a tree. I looked again. Yes, it was my tree! I recalled that it was a fruit tree of some type but I could not remember what kind of fruit it bore, *perhaps cherry or apple?* I had often watched it out my bedroom window and now I recognized the familiar shape of the branches against the sky and recalled that this was the tree that my father had planted when I was born. Miraculously it still stood; both of us had endured. It seemed significant, even symbolic. I noticed a place were the dirt looked a little darker and bent over and ran my bare nails across the spot. The dirt was soft enough to scrabble out with my fingers. I saw a glint of something gold, and dug harder.

It was my grandfather's gold watch! Caked with dirt, but his watch nonetheless. I would have known it anywhere; I fondly remembered the fine gold chain and how he would slip the watch into the pocket of his vest when he put on his fine clothes for weddings or Bar Mitzvahs. I dug deeper, and uncovered my mother's gold earrings, then her wedding ring.

These familiar objects reminded me with a stabbing pain of the dear ones who had once worn them and would never wear them again. I remembered that day the Nazis had ordered us to hand over our gold and our fur coats. My father must have dug this hole and hidden these treasures in the hope that someone in our family might survive to return and find them. It was all so incredible that after all that I had been through I had returned and found these family heirlooms.

"In spite of the exuberance of this discovery, I felt life drain out of me. They were gone. Each and every one of them. My family. The whole district, my entire community. Gone! Where could I turn, where could I go? *I am alone,* I thought, *alone in the world with no one!*" A numbing coldness settled on my heart as I trudged back to Wanda's barely able to lift my feet from the dust. The Czevchuks put their arms around me, but the shock and trauma of the previous five years settled around me like an unwelcome friend and I could hardly respond. They fed me, but my stomach rejected the food, and I became ill. I had no energy, no will to live.

The Czevchuks managed to persuade a passing doctor to see me. It was a crazy time. The doctor had retreated with the Russians and was now making her way back to Poland, back to her town of Katowice, but she stopped in Skalat long enough to examine me. I looked terrible, so gray, that she said she was surprised I had lived through the war. "You need to rest and recover," she said. The Russians were already clamoring for me to return to my old job at the bank, but the kind doctor wrote a letter saying that I was not well and could not work.

For several months, I did very little. I was lost in my grief, and though the Czevchuks encouraged me to hope, I felt that all I had hoped for—that someone in my family would come back to me—had eluded me. I could not climb out of my sadness. I searched the facial features of everyone I met, hoping to find a familiar face, but only heard each day about more friends, old boyfriends and cherished girlfriends who had died. None of my Jewish friends came back; they were all killed.

For so long I had dreamed of being reunited with my parents, and now I had to face the sad reality. I only hoped that my sister Pearl had made it to the United States, and if so, I knew she would be trying desperately to find out if anyone was left. And I had relatives in Canada. My mother's sister had moved to Toronto years before, and although I had never seen her, I had heard much about her. It was often said to me "You are the image of your Aunt Balsky." I gave much thought as to how I could establish contact with these relatives in another world, but it was not easy. The communists frowned on anyone who tried to get in touch with the already distrusted Americans, so I dared not do anything openly. I kept my thoughts to myself, but was determined to find a way to reach them.

By March 1944, the Russians were firmly in control of Poland. D-day was still three months away, and in other parts of Europe the war would still rage for more than a year. Conditions were not so good for us either, as the Russians were stern taskmasters. But at least there was not the daily threat of discovery and death. I was no longer in hiding, I had a job waiting for me and there was the tantalizing hope of reconnecting with my distant family. Luxuries were unobtainable, and we all concentrated on getting enough to eat and keeping warm and reasonably dressed. As everywhere in times of shortage, a vibrant black market sprang into being. Wanda's brother was highly involved, as he had gained the trust of the local farmers for his fairness in sharing everything during the war.

The Czevchuks had plenty of food through Bronak's "connections" and made sure I was included in this bounty. During the German occupation Bronak had managed to operate a clandestine butcher's business—including the pig they had hidden in bed with me. Bronak had always shared anything he managed to salvage with the neighbors, and they all trusted him. Under the Russians, his little business continued. Whenever a farmer could raise an extra animal, or there were extra eggs or other commodities, Bronak would arrange to make connections with people who wanted these things and had the cash to pay for them. It was a successful business, all run quietly behind the back of the Russian occupiers.

After a few months of rest, I returned to my job at the bank, and also began helping Bronak with his "business." The entire town used the bank, so I saw everyone. A customer only had to mention their longing for fresh meat, and I would whisper that I might be able to help them and put them in contact with Bronak. I also looked after the money for Bronak—receiving payment for the meat and putting it in a special account for him—without the authorities catching wind of what we were up to, something that was not easy in a communist country. I made a little extra money myself through this, and I put it all carefully away.

9

A Familiar Face

One day Bronak came to me with wonderful news. In the course of his "business" he often visited far flung farms, and in one of these he had heard a name that he had heard mentioned by me. It was Miss Sprenca! Of course he did not know if it was the same person, but there was a Miss Sprenca living at this remote farm, and it might be her. The next time he went there, I went with him— I was so excited at the thought of seeing someone who had been close to me in the old days, but I dared not hope for too much. To my delight, it was *my* Miss Sprenca— looking somewhat older and careworn, but alive!

She was overjoyed to see me and we immediately settled down for a long talk. She had left Skalat with no idea of where to go, just wanting to get as far away from town as possible. At first, she lived on berries and things she could find, eventually coming to a farm, a long way from anywhere. The people who lived there had been quite glad to have her help; she was an extra pair of hands to help with their many children, including a mentally retarded son.

Sprenca was terrified to admit she was Jewish, and had been enormously grateful that this family let her stay with them. She had worked hard, teaching the children to read and write and was particularly helpful with the retarded boy. I knew from personal experience that she had near limitless patience—I had taxed those limits myself! She had managed to teach this boy and he was much better, although he would never be normal. Then Sprenca told me that as the family had been very kind to her, and she owed them everything, she had agreed to marry the retarded son so she would be able to look after him.

I was horrified! Miss Sprenca was an intellectual who read a great deal, spoke several languages, and was highly intelligent. I could not contemplate her living the rest of her life miles away from the culture she loved, with people who, although no doubt kind and worthy, were not the intellectual equals she needed. In the pre-war days I had thought of Sprenca as "old"; in reality she was only a couple of years older than my sister Pearl. My parents had employed her as my governess when she had just graduated, and I now realized that she too had many years ahead of her.

"Sprenca," I pleaded, "You can't do this. You must come back to Skalat with me. We will share a room, and you can easily get a job. They need people. You cannot stay here miles from anywhere."

But she would not listen—she was too afraid to face real life again. "These people have been kind to me," she kept saying, "I am safe here. No one can find me."

I had to leave with Bronak, but I said I would soon be back, and made her promise that she would do nothing about the marriage until I came again. She agreed and I left; I knew she would not break her word to me. I had to find some way to keep her from ruining her life, but even more, she was the familiar face I had been searching for and now that I had found her, I was desperate to have her near.

The next week I persuaded Bronak to take me back. "I was so glad to find you," I told her. "After all I have been through I could not bear to be back in Skalat, so alone, with no one of my own. I am so lonely. I am beginning to think that after everything I just can't go on."

"But Fanie, you are so strong," Sprenca replied. "You can manage alone. You have done so much. You have endured so much. All I could do was hide here."

"But Sprenca," I told her, looking very plaintive and in fact near tears, "There is nothing else. All my family is gone. You are the nearest thing I have. My mother would expect you to help me, and now you will desert me, too."

"Fanie, do you really need me?" she asked. "I am terrified of leaving this refuge, but I know I do have a duty to you."

I cried and clung to her and we said we would care for each other. Sprenca packed her pathetically few belongings and we said goodbye to the family who had sheltered her, promising to keep in touch and return to see them as often as we could.

I am sure they were sorry to lose Sprenca, who had helped them so much, but they probably also realized that she too had a life, and staying there and marrying their much younger, retarded son was not fair to her. So we returned together to Skalat.

10

Expanding Our "Family"

After finding Miss Sprenca and persuading her to live with me, my spirits began to lift. It was easy to find a job for Sprenca. She spoke several languages, including Russian, quite fluently, and could write grammatically correct sentences as well. After all, I had done quite well with my skills, all of which I had learned from her. She got a job in the courthouse and we found a room where we could set up a home together. It was not luxurious, and we were rather cramped, but it was ours. With both of us bringing in a wage, we managed quite well. I made a little extra by facilitating Bronak in his clandestine butcher business, and I began to set aside the money I saved.

I was determined that one day I would get out of this life and contact my relations in the outside world. However, I was careful to keep this secret, as we were in an area that was very strictly controlled by the Russians. We did hear that other areas had more lenient administrations, and people there were allowed to contact the agencies that were attempting to reunite families, but this was completely forbidden in our area.

People began to trickle back into town. One day I was delighted to meet a distant cousin of my father's, Rabbi Schechter, who had been conscripted into the Russian army when they first arrived. He had spent the war on the Russian front, and had married a Russian girl. He was one of the fortunate survivors.

One day Miss Sprenca told me she had run into another family, the Sas family, who had told her an interesting story about attending a funeral of an old Catholic friend of theirs. Apparently, at the funeral the boy who carried the communion bread looked very familiar. They thought he might be a Jewish child who had been taken in by a Catholic family.

This story haunted Sprenca, and she would not rest until we had gone to see the family and heard their story. As soon as I saw the boy, I could see a strong resemblance to a Jewish family, the Bronsteins whom we had known before the war. The family looking after the boy opened up and told us the story. His entire family had been taken away, and they found him wandering alone, not knowing what to do. He must have been four or five years old at the time. They took him home, gave him a new name, as his own name "Chaim" would be dangerous. They brought him up with their own children. They realized he was Jewish, but of course wanted to hide it, and as they said, they knew nothing about the Jewish religion, so could not give him any instruction.

Sprenca decided at once that we must take responsibility for this boy. Despite our cramped quarters, we made room for Chaim. Sprenca, of course, would deal with his education, and I would buy his clothes, and find him little jobs in the bank to earn a few kopeks. He was an engaging child, and my coworkers enjoyed having him around. We both shared the food bills. We were a little family and went on happily for a while.

This state of affairs, however, could not continue. I had forgotten what a very tidy person Sprenca was—and I was anything but. There were three of us living in a small room, and Sprenca was always scolding me for leaving my things everywhere. She had always had to remind me to tidy up when she was my governess, and although it wasn't too bad when we lived in a large house, now it seemed obsessive.

We tried not to argue too much in front of Chaim, but it became obvious that we would have to do something. We were both getting more independent now, meeting all sorts of people, and enjoying others company again, and no longer needed each other. I was beginning to long for my independence and when I found a small room that I could afford, we both felt very relieved. We agreed that Chaim should live with Sprenca, but I would keep up my share in his support. Chaim loved his lessons with Sprenca and was learning rapidly. He was turning out to be a very clever child. I moved into my own little place, but continued to see a great deal of Sprenca and Chaim.

Despite the fact that the regime in Skalat was very tightly run and communication with the outside was not allowed, all sorts of news filtered through. Sprenca was particularly good at ferreting out information. For instance, she learned that in other locations, Jewish agencies were arranging to take orphaned children. Somehow she found out that Chaim had relatives who were looking for him. She immediately began teaching him Hebrew, in the hope that one day we would be able to reunite him with his family.

11

A Tall Soldier

I was being given more responsibility at the bank, and one of my jobs was to go to neighboring towns to pick up paper, ink, pens and pencils, which were always in short supply. It gave me a chance to see other places and try to find a way to move to a more tolerably run zone. I discovered that the only people who were given permits to move to other zones were soldiers returning from the Russian front.

One day I was sent to Lemberg, a neighboring town, for supplies for the bank. Trains were not punctual, and there were always long waits at the station. On this occasion there was a group of soldiers waiting for the train, who were being transferred from a hospital in Kiev. One of the soldiers caught my eye, and we began a conversation. He was tall and thin, and I thought rather good-looking. I discovered he was Jewish, and came from Copernicus Street in the town of Berezno, about 200 miles north of Skalat. The Germans had taken his family during the war, but he had managed to escape to join the Partisans. He fought with them for some time and was actually a member of the very group that had so briefly driven the Germans from Skalat. His group of Partisans had eventually joined up with the Russians, and been conscripted into the Russian army. He had been injured, losing two fingers on his right hand, and had just been released from the hospital in Kiev.

He was en route to Bitov, which was in a different zone—one that was much more relaxed than Skalat. I was quite envious.

There was a long wait, so as we stood, we talked. I told him much of my own story, and he told me that all his family had been killed, and like me, he was quite alone. His family had been in the meat business before the war, dealing with both Kosher and non-Kosher meat. He had been very useful to the Partisans when they were living in the forest, as he could butcher animals they got from local farms in exchange for vodka they stole from government liquor plants. He could also prepare and cook all kinds of meat. I told him of my fierce longing to get out of Poland, and how difficult things were in Skalat compared to other places. We opened up our hearts to each other, and I was quite sad when my train arrived, and we went our separate ways.

Ten days later the tall soldier, whose name was Jerzy Gusz, unexpectedly walked into the bank where I worked. He had managed to get a travel pass for a couple of days, and we agreed to meet after I was done for the day. "I have been making inquiries for you," he told me, "because I realized how anxious you are to leave here."

I was surprised and touched that a stranger should go to such trouble for me, and amazed to see that he had a sheaf of documents with him. I knew how tight security was, but he had checked out everything. "I can only get documents for a very close relative," he told me. "Only a mother, a sister, or a wife. I had hoped I might call you a cousin, but that is not close enough."

We were required to carry so many identification papers; there was no way I could pretend to be his sister. I looked up into his kind eyes, "I could be your wife," I said, smiling.

Jerzy's eyes met mine and he smiled, "Yes, you could be my wife."

It seemed crazy, but for two lonely souls, bereft of family, it was a chance for a new beginning. Jerzy looked at his bandaged hand and I knew he felt tarnished by his missing fingers. I only knew that from the first moment I saw him at the railway station I had found him a very attractive man. We had talked for hours, sharing our hearts and minds. I took his hand in mine, and our eyes met again. We would go forward together into whatever God had for us.

"I need to go to the hospital in Bitov," Jerzy told me, "So the doctors can examine my hand. We must marry immediately." He was right. Although he had been discharged from the hospital in Kiev, he needed to be under a doctor's care until his hand healed completely. I did not want to tell the bank I was leaving. They might have created difficulties as bookkeepers were in short supply and we were expected to put the good of the "people" ahead of any individual desires.

We went to the local registry office to obtain the necessary permits. Thankfully no one questioned us. The registrar took a look at Jerzy's uniform and his bandaged hand, recognized that he was a solider returning from the Russian front and was more than willing to accommodate our request. After a short wait we had a wedding license.

It was much harder telling Sprenca! She was horrified. "You are Fanie Steinbock," she told me—as if I needed reminding. "You cannot run off and marry just anybody! What would your parents say?" I reminded her gently that my parents were unfortunately in no position to say anything, which made her even angrier. "Yes," she cried. "And I am here in their place. You said you needed me. I forbid you to marry this stranger."

Oddly enough, Sprenca's antagonism made me all the more determined to marry Jerzy. The more she protested, the more my decision seemed the right one. "Sprenca," I urged her, "Just think what this means to us all. From Bitov I will be able to contact the Jewish agencies and find out about our relatives. We know they are looking for us and we will be able to let them know we are still alive. We will be able to reunite Chaim with his family!"

Instead of pacifying her, this made Sprenca cry all the harder. "You are selling yourself for us," She wailed. "I would never have come to look after you had I known I would fail so miserably in my duty. I cannot let you go off with this stranger to a new town where you know no one."

Eventually I gave up trying to placate Sprenca. Time was running out, and we had a lot to do to arrange the wedding before Jerzy and I had to leave. We both wished for a religious ceremony, and went to Rabbi Schechter to see if it could be arranged. To our delight, he was most enthusiastic. After the scene with Sprenca I was feeling very shaken, and Rabbi Schechter did much to allay my worries. He agreed with Sprenca that it was all very hasty, but under the circumstances he could understand the necessity. He took an immediate liking to Jerzy, and privately told me that he instinctively felt he was a good man. "I have had a lot of experience with people," he told me. "Sometimes one has to make a snap decision. Who knows, perhaps the meeting between you was ordained by God. You must follow what your heart tells you."

That made me feel much better, as did the excitement our announcement generated. The Rabbi's wife and another cousin, Hinde, who had returned to Skalat, were determined to rustle up a wedding feast. We set the date for May 15, 1945, a date that all (except Sprenca) declared to be propitious. Hinde and the Rabbi's wife performed miracles. Nothing has ever tasted better than the chicken soup and latkes they served. Everybody felt that it was wonderful to have a joyous occasion after all the sorrow. The war in Europe had finally ended the week before with the German's surrender on May 7, 1945, so there were many reasons to celebrate. The only dark spot was Sprenca, who cried noisily all through the ceremony. Jerzy has never forgiven her!

Afterwards we had to rush off to get exit papers that showed my new status before the office closed. We wanted to leave as soon as possible as I was afraid we had been seen at the registry office, and the bank might try to stop me from leaving. Once in another zone, they would have no jurisdiction over me and I would be safe. As soon as we had the papers, Mr. and Mrs. Jerzy Gusz boarded the train for Bitov.

12

Making Plans for a New Life

It was strange being addressed as Mrs. Gusz, but comforting to know that I was now part of a family. Once in Bitov, our top priority was to register as a married couple so we could get suitable accommodation. All through the town, piles of rubble marked the spots where houses once stood. Housing was in short supply and the authorities ordered the German residents to take in Polish survivors, including Jews like us. By the end of the day the housing office had given us a room in the home of a German family who not only gave us a large bedroom but shared their kitchen and living rooms as well.

Jerzy's ravaged hand was treated at the hospital and while he healed, we lived on the little money each of us had put aside; and I found ways of making a small income bartering produce, jam, clothing—anything I could get my hands on. We did not want to settle into Bitov permanently; although it was less authoritarian than Skalat, Bitov was still under Soviet control and not what we wanted. It was considerably easier, however, to get permits to move about and after just a few months in Bitov, we got a permit to move to Waldenburg, another town further west. Like Bitov, this town had also once been part of Germany but was now ceded to Poland. It was closer to the western border, just 60 kilometers northeast of

Stuttgart, and much more open. In Waldenburg we were able to make direct contact with the Jewish agencies.

We had registered our names with HIAS, the Hebrew Immigrant Air Society, as wanting to leave Poland. They told us that it might take some time to arrange, so we settled into life in Waldenburg, renting a two-bedroom apartment where we managed to open a little store on the main floor. There was almost no cash in town as the German marks issued under the Nazi regime were now worthless, so everything in the store was bartered. A family might bring in a man's suit or a gold bracelet, which they traded for butter, coffee or the fabric to make their growing daughter a new dress. We did very well. I had a knack for obtaining much desired produce from the local farmers and Jerzy was very good with people. The shop expanded into quite a large store that produced enough income to cover our living expenses as well as to set aside a considerable sum for our hoped for emigration. We never lost sight of our main objective—to get back to the free world.

We had only been in Waldenburg a few months when I discovered that I was pregnant. I was quite upset, as we were anxious to get away and were afraid that a child might complicate our lives at this stage. When Martin arrived, however, on February 21, 1946, nine months and a week after our wedding, we were both thrilled. His arrival made us all the more determined to ensure a good life for our little family. I remember holding him in my arms as I recalled that terrible night when I crouched in an attic listening to cries of "*Judenfrei!*"

"No, my baby," I murmured to him, "Even with all their might, they could not destroy us. We are here." I was reminded again of the "onion" remark that had ruined Emil Summerstein's political career. Sadly many layers, most of my family, had been peeled away, but this precious remnant was the beginning of a new dynasty. And our erstwhile destroyers were indeed shedding tears.

From the agencies I learned that my sister and my aunt, as well as Jerzy's uncle in Winnipeg, were trying to contact us, but we were unable to receive mail as the agency was not permitted to bring in any direct messages from outside. It was clear that we would not lack sponsors to get our visas to the U.S.A. or Canada, but in the meantime we had to be patient and concentrate on Martin.

Eventually we got our instructions. We were to cross into Czechoslovakia at a certain border crossing in the company of a party of Greeks. These Greek men had been taken from their homeland by the Nazis during the war and forced to work on farms that were lying fallow in Germany, because virtually all the able-bodied Germans were in the military. Now that the war was over, the Greeks were eager to return home and we hoped to cross the border with them. The Jewish agency gave us falsified Greek papers, and cautioned us not to utter a word as neither of us spoke Greek. We decided to go through the border control separately to lessen the temptation to inadvertently speak to each other. We changed all our money into gold, which I sewed into the hem of my dress and the baby's clothes.

I carried Martin, who was a chubby baby to start with and now even more heavy with the gold sewn into his clothes. My own clothes were also weighted down by the gold and as we approached the border control, my arms ached. *Was that a child's buggy abandoned on the side of the road?* I looked around, but saw no owner, so as our Greek party trudged on, I decided to take it as a gift from heaven, and with a sigh of relief, laid Martin into it. That made things much easier. I took it as a sign of God's favor, and went on confidently.

The customs officer was surprisingly pleasant. I noticed that he wore a large cross around his neck and was obviously a devout Catholic. He picked up Martin who was a beautiful child with golden curls and big blue eyes. "A lovely child," he said fondly. "Just like our Savior." He was clearly a family man who loved children. At any other time I would have delighted in the admiration, but all I wanted to do was get through this checkpoint. I smiled and nodded, careful not to say anything or let him know that I understood what he was saying. Surreptitiously I pinched Martin's bottom hoping that he would cry or do something unpleasant, but he continued to gurgle charmingly. After what seemed like an eternity, he returned the baby to the buggy, having missed the gold pieces sewn into Martin's diaper, thank heaven! I pushed the baby on through into comparative freedom.

13

Escape Across Europe

Once safely across the border, I looked around for Jerzy who I saw in the distance. He was a little worried as I had been longer than he expected, and he was surprised to see the buggy. I told him what had happened, and as we walked on, we saw a man running towards us. "God bless you! God bless you!" he shouted. "Where did you get that buggy?" he queried as soon as he was within speaking distance. I told him the story: that I had just found it by the road, and taken it as a gift from heaven. He smiled. "Now let me show you something," he said. He tenderly lifted Martin out, and handed him to me. He then pushed down on the bottom of the buggy, which opened to reveal a cache of jewelry, silver and gold. We gasped. "These are my family heirlooms," he said. "We kept all of it buried during the war, and carefully hid it afterwards to provide a foundation for us in the New World if we could make it. I made this hidden compartment in the buggy, and intended to bring it through. Then as I neared the border, my heart failed. They were searching so many people—just suppose these treasures were found! I knew I would face a return to prison, possibly even death, so I decided to abandon my goods and trust my own two hands for the future. Better to be poor and free."

I felt faint. *What if the guard had found all this*! He would never have believed my story.

"Please take anything you want," the owner of the buggy said, his eyes now streaming with tears of joy. "I thank you with all my heart and am truly grateful for this miracle."

"Please may I keep the buggy?" I asked immediately. It had been wonderful not having to carry my heavy baby. Who cared about gold and silver when ones arms ached like mine had done?

"Of course you may," he replied. "And you must have something else as well to show my gratitude."

We wanted nothing. At this moment all that mattered was that we were safe and finally outside the stifling Soviet regime. After that incident I was more than ever convinced that God was with us, but our journey to freedom had only just begun. We had been told to stay with the Greek contingent until we reached Pocking, Germany where there was a refugee camp with facilities for obtaining visas. There were various agencies established there with the express purpose of helping people reunite, so that was where we had to go.

We were in Czechoslovakia, but that was merely the first step—albeit a most important one. We were to go on to Vienna, and from there to Paris. It was a roundabout route, but one that had been carefully planned for our party. We had to be sure not to cross back into the Soviet-controlled zones, and be sure that our passes would be valid when we wished to cross borders. Traveling by train through Europe was very depressing. Everywhere we saw the results of the bombing and the fighting. Out of this destruction, the people were struggling to return to normality—to rebuild from the rubble, find a livelihood, and make a life again. We reached Passau, Germany near the border of Austria, but our stay there was very brief as I had an allergic reaction to the numerous evergreen trees, and felt very ill. From there we went on to Regensburg, and eventually Pocking, Germany. Finally, three years after we first left Skalat, we were under U.N. and U.S. jurisdiction.

Our party split up there, as people were taking different routes.

Several were going on to Israel. Jerzy had originally wanted to go there, but knowing we had family in Canada and America, we decided to try to get a visa to those two countries first. The refugee camp was housed in on a former military base. Each family was assigned two rooms in the barracks; one was used as a kitchen and the other a bedroom. The base was in the countryside outside town with lovely trees all around and there was a twice-daily bus to take us into town. Even so, I was glad that we would not be there long.

To our delight there already were letters and parcels awaiting us. It had been impossible to forward them into Poland, but many of the agencies were aware of our group's movements, and knew that our intended destination was Pocking.

For the first time I learned that my sister, Pearl, had survived her perilous journey and was alive. She had reached America after being held over in England for a short while when the war broke out. She was living in New Jersey and was married to a fellow Polish immigrant, Sam Schlanger. They had met and become engaged when Sam was still in the American Army. He had been wounded in Japan, and Pearl had flown over there and married him while he was still in the hospital. He was apparently quite well to do, as he was a partner with his four brothers in an oil business. Pearl assured me that they were longing to have us with them until we were well established. After all I had been through, she wrote, I deserved a wonderful new life, and she and Sam would see that we had it.

Pearl had also contacted Aunt Leah Balsky in Toronto, Canada, who was equally anxious to help and had also sent letters and parcels. They had both advertised in Canada and in the U.S. and had found out that Jerzy's grandmother and one uncle had escaped the Holocaust. His grandmother had lived in Detroit, Michigan, but had recently died, while the uncle lived in Winnipeg, Canada. There were letters from Jerzy's Uncle Raber, too. He had gone to Toronto to advise Aunt Balsky, and consulted an immigration lawyer there who had given Aunt Balsky advice on how to apply for visas. He told her to say that I was her sister, as the closer the relationship the better. We were a little concerned that Jerzy's missing fingers might prove a detriment in getting a visa, but Uncle Raber signed all the documents guaranteeing himself as a full sponsor and agreeing to cover any expenses we might incur.

Now it was only a matter of time. There were literally thousands of people haunting the agencies, trying to trace their families, and we had to wait our turn. Our families were most generous and we also received parcels of food and clothing from the Red Cross as well as CARE packages (boxes of fruit, jam, canned meats, and soup) financed by our relatives in America. We sold everything that we did not need on the black market to get money to live on.

We had to undergo grueling questioning to ensure we were not trying to use someone else's identification. We spent endless hours at the embassies, both American and Canadian. As time went on, I felt more drawn to Canada. The United States seemed so huge, teeming with people and fiercely competitive, whereas Canada seemed to move at a gentler pace. Also we both had relatives in Canada, which we pictured as being near each other, not knowing that Winnipeg is more than 2000 kilometers from Toronto.

I was also a little wary of Pearl's idea of a "wonderful life." From what I remembered of her, I thought it would involve much socializing, glamorous clothes and that sort of thing. It had never been my style, and somehow I did not visualize Jerzy fitting into it either. I did not voice these misgivings aloud, however, and we vowed to accept whichever visa was granted first.

While waiting in Pocking, Martin was stricken with a childhood ailment and was seen by a Polish doctor who worked at the American Embassy. He became quite a close friend as he welcomed every opportunity to speak Polish, and was extremely helpful to us on several occasions, including finding a spot for Martin in a nursery school so I could wait in the interminable lines. We were worried that Jerzy might be turned down because of his missing fingers, but the doctor assured us that he would sign a health certificate that would make it clear that Jerzy was not disabled in spite of his injury.

Many other people we met were also waiting for visas, and we became friends. We were sitting on a bench at the U.S. Embassy, waiting for them to call our name when we struck up a conversation with a couple sitting next to us. The wife said they hoped to go to Newark, where she had a cousin. She pulled out some photos, and to our amazement, one was a picture of us!—a copy of one I had sent Pearl. The lady's cousin was Pearl's husband and my brother-in-law! I introduced them to my doctor friend in the U.S. Embassy and he was able to help them get a visa to the U.S. so they could emigrate there.

Everyday we waited. Martin kept us both busy, and his blond good looks made him quite a favorite at the embassies. Time hung heavy on our hands, but at least we knew our applications were creeping forward. Finally one day, after ten months of waiting, it happened: both embassies called on the same day! Now which one to chose? "I would like to go to Canada so I can meet my Aunt Leah Balsky," I told Jerzy. I had never met Aunt Leah, but for years people in our village had told me that I looked like her, I talked like her, and even walked like her. Now I wanted to see her for myself. I considered going to my sister in New Jersey, but did not feel drawn in that direction. We had once been so different; would time have changed that? I did not think so. We would go to Aunt Leah and Canada, a decision I have never regretted, as Canada has become my home and a defining part of who I am.

1930 | With sister Pearl and my father's sister,
Aunt Szencia

1939 | With my mother and sister, Pearl

1939 | *Pearl and me*

1939 | *Outside our home in Skalat*

1948 | *In Pocking*

With Jerry and Martin before leaving Hamburg for Canada

1973 | *Embarking on trip to Israel*

By the Western Wall in Jerusalem

With Jerry outside our store at
122 Dundas Street

With Prime Minister John Turner

With Prime Minister John Turner

With Lieutenant Governor Lincoln Alexander at a reception

1985 | *Celebrating with Premier-elect
David Peterson at his 1985 victory*

*With David Peterson and Lieutenant Governor
Hilary Weston*

With Joe Fontana, MP, and Pat O'Brien, MP

Cutting the cake at the July 1st swearing in of new immigrants

Radio host Bill Brady making a toast at our golden wedding anniversary

Jerry and me

Signing up Liberal members

With Granddaughter, Danielle

With grandson Michael at his Bar Mitzvah

With Dalton McGuinty, Premier of Ontario

At an exhibition commemorating Holocaust survivors, London Art Gallery

2002 | At presentation of Queen's Medal

With Mayor Tom Gosnell and Laurel Gosnell

With Prime Minister Jean Chretien and Mayor Dianne Haskett

At dedication of Jerry and Fanny Goose library of Judaica at
Chabad Lubavitch Centre

With Steven, Martin, Heather, and Michael at Jerry's 80th birthday

2004 | *JNF Negev dinner in our honor*

With Mayor Anne Marie DeCicco-Best

Fred Kingsmill and me on Dundas Street

At the opening of the 'Fanny and Jerry Goose Dining Room' at Baycrest

With Ellen McKim and Prime Minister Paul Martin

With Jerry

On the Jim Chapman television show

Family celebration, from left: Our inlaws, Mr. and Mrs. Campbell, daughter-in-law, Michelle Campbell, son Steven (Garrison), daughter-in-law, Heather Goose, son Martin Goose, granddaughter, Rebecca Goose

Martin and Heather Goose

Steven Garrison and Michelle Campbell

Sons Martin and Steven

Back row: Granddaughter, Rebecca; Heather and Martin; Steven and Michelle;
Front row: Granddaughter, Danielle; Me and Jerry; grandson Michael

With Prime Minister Paul Martin

With Nancy Poole and Betty Lang at fundraiser for Hardy Geddes Home

At Negev dinner with Mrs Posluns (President of JNF)

Watching Christmas parade with Morris Della Costa, Michelle, London Fire
Chief Hodgins, Megan Walker, and Steve

Receiving downtown award with Councillor Cheryl Miller and John Nash

In Miami with other survivors from Skalat

With Marvin (Pearl's son) and Elizabeth Schlange

With Major General Lewis McKenzie and
Frances Shapiro

*With local philanthropist Miggsie Lawson at
St Joseph's fundraising dinner*

At our golden wedding anniversary

Janet Fridman, with husband, Professor Emeritus Gerald Fridman

With Janet Fridman

14

Our New Life Begins

Although we had been informed that our visas were granted, we still had to go to Hamburg, Germany to pick them up and would sail from there to Canada. I said goodbye to the helpful Polish doctor, who was quite disappointed that we were not going to the U.S., and we boarded the train to Hamburg.

Hamburg was an eye opener. The shops were full of fine European wares, a huge contrast to Pocking where one had to scrounge for anything nice. The prices were also very reasonable. We had done very well with our little store in Waldenburg, and managed to make a little bit of money bartering goods in Pocking as well. We were advised that first-rate china and crystal were not to be had in North America so I embarked on a delightful shopping spree, being careful to set aside the money for a down payment on a house once we arrived in Canada.

I had the most marvelous time, as I had always loved silver, china and crystal, and a wide selection was readily available. The highlight of my spree came in an elegant china shop where I was shown an exquisite 24-place dinner service that had been ordered by the infamous Hermann Goering—but it had never been picked up! It was a lovely flowered pattern with shades of pink flowers on bone rimmed in gold, and its history made it impossible to resist. I bought it, and still have it. I also bought presents to take to my relatives in the New World. We were not going to arrive empty-handed.

On August 15, 1949, more than four years after we married and left Skalat, we set sail for Quebec on the *Queen Mary*, a large ocean liner. After the happy interlude in Hamburg, the journey was a great contrast. Both Jerzy and I were horribly seasick, and could hardly bear the journey. Three and a half-year-old Martin, however, whom we had begun calling "Zenya", loved the ship, running around full of lively curiosity. I was much too sick to look after him. I could only hope that someone else would keep an eye on him, as I was entirely at the mercy of my roiling stomach. Two days before we landed in Quebec, we reached the quieter waters of the St. Lawrence River and I began to feel a little better. It was then I met a Polish lady by the name of Janet who had watched over Zenya while the rolling seas had confined me to my bed. She was traveling alone, on her way to Halifax, Nova Scotia. I thanked her and gave her a pair of nylon stockings I had purchased in Hamburg. She was thrilled as they were a product quite sought after at the time.

When our boat pulled into the dock at Quebec City, we were somewhat travel worn, but very excited to be on Canadian soil. We boarded a train for Toronto, and after an eight-hour journey we at last reached our destination where we received a hero's welcome. Aunt Leah was on the platform to greet us along with her daughter, Sarah, and her granddaughter, Marilyn. It was wonderful to be surrounded by so much love. Everyone was bearing gifts and wanted to entertain us. As some of our packages had been shipped separately from us, I was so delighted when they finally arrived and we were able to reciprocate a little. Pearl and Uncle Raber were constantly phoning from New Jersey and Winnipeg, demanding to know when they would meet us.

My first sight of the Balsky home was a surprise. They had been in Canada a long time, and we thought that all North Americans were very rich, so their comfortable but quite ordinary home surprised us. I think that subconsciously, I had been expecting something like Castle Zadniesowka, an imposing structure on a hill surrounded by a moat, with an eight-foot high front door made of great slabs of wood, a great hall, and eight bedrooms.

Our first Sunday in Toronto, we were invited to a traditional Jewish wedding. It had been many years since either of us had attended a formal Jewish function, and we were curious to see what customs were followed in Canada. It was a very heart-warming experience for us both. I had vague memories of weddings from before the war, and it was wonderful to find that the young people were still married under a canopy by a rabbi in a black hat. The singing and dancing thrilled my heart and I was struck over and over again by the freedom to celebrate and make a little noise without fear. We thoroughly enjoyed every second, and felt very much a part of it. I was happy that the parcels from my Hamburg shopping spree had arrived and we were able to present the young couple with a glittering crystal bowl.

As soon as we got to Toronto, Pearl came from New Jersey to visit. I was excited to see her after ten years apart, and wondered what she would look like. To my surprise she looked exactly the same as I remembered her, hardly a day older, still blonde and immaculately groomed, a beautiful woman of great refinement. I was the one who had changed. I was no longer the wild tomboy she had left in Poland. I was now a woman – a wife and a mother. I was in good health but I felt I looked no younger than my elder sibling. *She was the fortunate one*, I thought, looking at her. *She got out before it was too late.*

I remembered how my mother had cried for Pearl. Almost everyone else in the family had favored me—Grandpa, Grandma, my aunt, and my father, but my mother had adored her ladylike daughter, Pearl. The local Skalat schools where I received my education had not been good enough for Pearl; my parents had sent her to the university in Lemberg. She was also too fine for the shops in Skalat and made regular forays to posh shops in Lemberg, coming home by train, her arms full of parcels.

Once I snuck into her room after she had come home late from a long shopping expedition and put on the clothes she had purchased the day before. I was only ten years old, so the navy blue silk dress, with the delicate floral print on the bodice, dragged a bit on the ground as I wobbled out the front door in her new high heeled shoes, a white panama hat with pink silk flowers atop my head. "Look what Pearl bought in Lemberg," I called out to the neighbors.

Two days later, when Pearl donned her ensemble for the first time, the neighbors laughingly informed her that they already seen her finery—on me. An outraged Pearl marched home to complain to Mother, who scolded me, "Fanie, you are not to do this. Those things are Pearl's!"

Now that Pearl was standing in front of me, this memory and many painful memories crowded in. Pearl wanted to know everything that had happened, but it was soon clear that she had no concept of the horrors we had endured. She seemed amazed that our house, indeed the entire district, had been destroyed, and wanted to know what had happened to our possessions. She kept asking about various items, and seemed surprised that I had no idea if they had been confiscated or destroyed. "But you were there, Fanie," she kept saying. "Surely you know if the Germans took our things or not. We might be able to trace them." She was particularly interested to know what had happened to a painting that had hung on the staircase. We both remembered it well—a study of Delilah cutting off Samson's hair. I have no idea whether it was valuable or not, but it did recall old times to us. "We must find that picture if possible," Pearl reiterated. "Try to remember Fanie. Did you see it on the wall again? Or see it carried out?"

It seemed impossible for her to grasp that we had been solely concerned with survival. The gold and the pictures had meant nothing to us in the overarching struggle to live, to endure the war and to survive. I had not even thought of the picture until she reminded me. I found it very sad that I was unable to relate more closely with my only sister, particularly as we were the only survivors of a wonderful home life. I realized that the intervening years and difference in our experiences had widened the gap between us. Wonderful as it was to see my sister again, I realized that it was best that we had chosen Canada as our home rather than joining Pearl in the U.S.

The stay in Toronto was most pleasant for Jerzy and me, but we were very anxious to get on with our lives and get established. It was always an unspoken worry between us that Jerzy's injured hand might stand in the way of his finding employment. It felt providential therefore when we read in the Jewish newspaper that the Kosher butcher in London, Ontario, southwest of Toronto, was looking for an assistant. Jerzy had been trained in the business with his family, and had practiced his skills while with the Partisans during the war. London was only 120 miles from Toronto, and a friend of my aunt was cousin to the Rabbi there. When we mentioned this to my aunt's friend, he immediately rang Rabbi Kirschenbaum to tell him about us. I had mentioned my concern that they might think Jerzy would not be able to do the job, but Rabbi Kirschenbaum assured us that he would speak to the butcher, Mr. Lapovich, and all would be okay. We went to London to arrange everything, and Jerzy was hired for $35.00 a week and all the meat we could eat!

Rabbi Kirschenbaum was very helpful and arranged for us to have a room with a Mrs. Jack for ten dollars a week. It was our first step on the road to independence. I immediately enrolled in English classes as the only English I spoke had been picked up as I went along and I wanted to improve. I had been properly instructed in the other languages I had learned, including proper grammar, but English grammar was tricky. Even today, I am not as fluent as I would like to be, but I always manage to make myself understood.

Once we moved to London, we joined the synagogue. I had a good grounding in our Jewish faith and traditions from my grandfather, but it was not as orthodox as Jerzy, who derived deep satisfaction from his religious practices. Through the synagogue, we met members of the community. We were somewhat cramped in our rented room, and were delighted when a lady in our synagogue, Mrs. Hoffman, offered us an apartment in her home at a rent we could afford. We were very happy there as the flat had more room for Martin who was now four and very active.

Jerzy was working hard, and I wanted something to do as well. I made a friend, Sarah Rottman, who earned a nice income selling clothes on commission for her cousin Sam Leach. She introduced me to him, and he offered to supply me with clothing if I would give him the cash in exchange for a percentage of each item I sold. I agreed saying, "Give me a sweater and I will see what I can do." I made 10 cents commission that day, and was thrilled.

I discovered that I enjoyed selling clothes, and was good at it. I related well to other new immigrants, and soon was making a nice income. I realized there was a great opportunity here as many of the immigrants did not speak English well and were uncomfortable going into shops. They would write down what they wanted me to bring them. I still remember, one man who wrote the word "jeans" on a slip of paper. "Jeans?" I did not know what they were, but my friend Sally soon set me straight. I soon learned where I could buy clothes directly from the factories in Toronto, and began making the two-hour journey by train to make my own purchases. I bought clothes that were on clearance and made a good profit. I wanted to expand into the rural areas surrounding the city where there were many new settlers, but I could not drive.

By this time, I was earning as much as Jerzy, and then quite unexpectedly he lost his job with the butcher. The shop was sold to new owners who were unwilling to retain a butcher with two missing fingers. I persuaded Jerzy to work with me and soon he was driving a red panel truck to the local farms. He was also a good salesman, and we began to do very well.

15

Becoming Fanny Goose

A month after we moved into Mrs. Hoffman's apartment, Jerzy was making his rounds and spied a house for sale near the factories that populated the east end of London. It was on York Street, right across from the Gair Company cardboard container factory and we immediately saw its potential: workers could shop in our store and save themselves the trip downtown. We bought the house and turned the downstairs living room into a store, which we filled with the kind of merchandise that would appeal to hard-working factory employees: work uniforms, jeans, casual clothes, Sunday dresses and suits, and children's toys. We sold clothes for the entire family, from dresses and pants to shoes and shirts. We rented out two of the bedrooms upstairs and lived in what remained: one of the upstairs bedrooms, which we shared with four-year-old Martin, the kitchen and the dining room. One of our roomers owned a restaurant nearby and the other drove a taxi.

A lawyer, Sam Lerner, arranged the purchase and proved to be a great friend. While we were buying the house, we discussed our ambitions with him, and he suggested that Jerzy Gusz was not a particularly good name for a clothing business in Canada. We asked him for ideas, and he said that Jerry Goose would sound much better. I must have made a face, as he then laughed, and said "Mother Goose is a well known character in children's fairy tales. They will recognize the name at once. If you don't mind being called 'Mother Goose', I think it would be a good name." We listened to him, and for more years than I care to remember I have been known, affectionately I hope, as "Mother Goose". He also pointed out that "Fanny" was more Canadian than "Fanie", and I would probably be called that anyway. He was right. We have been Fanny and Jerry since then, even though I sometimes regret the loss of my real name, which was pronounced Fanya, and I think much prettier than Fanny.

Pearl visited for a second time after we moved to London, this time bringing her two sons and her husband. She was quite keen to have us visit her in New Jersey, but I was afraid to leave Canada, afraid that we would not be let back in as we were not yet citizens. I told Sam Lerner this, and he immediately wrote a letter explaining that I was in the process of obtaining citizenship and that I was an upstanding citizen and property owner. Assured that I was quite safe, I made my first visit to America where I saw Pearl's beautiful new home in New Jersey. It was exquisitely decorated, with lavish furnishings and distinctive artwork—just what I had expected.

16

Branching Out

Our business was growing rapidly, and our country customers were beginning to come into London to buy from our shop. Our first customers on York St were a family called Parsons and they dealt with us faithfully for many years—in fact they had a saying that Christmas would not be Christmas without a shopping spree at Goose's Family Clothing!

We were doing so well that we began to think of the possibility of buying larger premises, and one day Jerry spotted a property for sale on Dundas Street East. There was a charming two-bedroom clapboard cottage on the land, but what drew Jerry's attention was the location—very near a number of factories including Kelloggs, Emco, and McCormicks—and on the main street in London.

Another advantage of the position was that there was a good school for Martin nearby. We hired workers to move the cottage to the back of the property and built a store in the front, with two apartments upstairs that rented out, and a shop below, which we rented to a beauty salon. Our family lived in the cottage, which made a cozy home for our two growing boys—Martin who was now nine and our second son Steven who was one and had just started to walk.

Our estimate of the potential of the Dundas location proved to be right. We were close to factories that paid good wages, which made it easy for the employees to shop with us. Long before other stores were open long hours, you could shop in our store, Goose Family Clothing, any hour of the day or night. If you tore your trousers at 11 o'clock at night, there would always be someone in our store to sell you a new pair.

We were so successful that we were soon able to purchase the property next-door, which we demolished so we could expand our store and add three more apartments upstairs. Jerry had given up his trips into the country as our rural customers now all came to us, and he needed to be full time in the shop.

Charles Ivey, one of London's most generous philanthropists, owned and operated the Emco factory very near our property. Although his firm specialized in manufacturing pipes for plumbing and heating, he took a great interest in our development, and came into the store several times before I realized who he was. He made many helpful suggestions and was always very kind and friendly.

He told us how much it pleased him to see new immigrants doing so well, and that the future of London was in the hands of people like us. He would come into the shop and watch us, and on some occasions when we were really busy he would serve a customer himself! I often wondered what those customers would think if they knew they were being attended by one of London's wealthiest men.

Another person who gave us great assistance was Richard Shapiro. He was the owner of much larger retail outlets than ours, but he would come over to us on Sunday and dress our shop window. He too was very interested in our progress.

After a few years we saw that things were changing in London. Discount stores were sprouting up, and the area of East London where we operated was being pushed out by downtown shops. I had always wanted a store downtown, and this ambition was realized when we bought 122 Dundas Street where we opened a larger shop, called J. Goose Family Clothing, that is still open today. One of the neighboring shops is Kingsmill's, one of London's most prestigious stores, and I felt a little overwhelmed at being in such close proximity. Fred Kingsmill who owns and runs the store is from an old London family, and I was afraid he might look on us as "upstart immigrants." Nothing could have been further from the truth; he was supportive from the outset, and has become one of our closest friends.

Once years later when I was in the hospital, he called Steven to see if there was anything he could do for me. After many calls, Steven thought of something— new slippers. That evening Fred arrived in my hospital room with five or six boxes containing a complete selection of slippers from the store.

Richard Shapiro introduced us to an agent, Sylvia Sharnow, who introduced us to wholesalers in Toronto. Before we met, Richard would tell Sylvia that she must get us the lowest prices possible, as "poor Mrs. Goose" was an immigrant who could not afford to pay high prices. One day I went into Toronto with Richard. I did not get there very often, and dressed myself up for the day out, wearing my best clothes and a newly acquired mink stole. When Richard introduced me to Sylvia, she took one look and said, "So this is POOR Mrs. Goose. I may have to revise my prices." Sylvia and I subsequently became good friends.

Pearl visited us several times. She came to both our son's Bar Mitzvahs, and of course we went her sons'. For her elder son's Bar Mitzvah I had purchased what I thought to be some very smart outfits in Toronto. When we arrived in New York, Pearl demanded to see what I planned to wear. She was quite horrified at my clothes, and insisted I come to her couturier. There was no time to have anything specially made, but she picked out a couple of elegant gowns for me. *How absolutely beautiful!* I thought. When I saw the prices I nearly had a heart attack, but Pearl insisted I have them as a gift. I had never seen such exquisitely made garments, and although they no longer fit, I still keep them in the back of my wardrobe. Needless to say, they were hardly suitable for my modest life in London, Ontario.

We attended another Bar Mitzvah in America that made us very happy. The Sas family, who long ago had found Chaim, had also moved to the U.S. and was doing well. They told us that Chaim was in Israel, where he was a professor at the University of Tel Aviv. He sent me a copy of one of his books, in Hebrew, which I cannot read, but my heart swelled with pride when I opened the book and saw the beautiful characters.

Sprenca too came to America. She contacted me through Pearl, and told me that she had married a cousin who had turned up after the war, and they had been able to find relatives to sponsor them in the U.S. She also had two sons. We often spoke on the telephone, usually when Jerry was out. He never forgave Sprenca for crying all through our wedding.

We celebrated the Bar Mitzvah of our elder son, Martin, at the synagogue on Horton Street near the downtown, which we had joined when we first came to London. It was an Orthodox synagogue, and at that time, the only synagogue in London. However, as the community moved further north, it was no longer a convenient location and the Jewish community decided to build a new synagogue in North London on the corner of Adelaide and Huron Streets. In this way, Or Shalom came into being. Steven had his Bar Mitzvah there. We too moved to North London, purchasing our home in Harrison Crescent where I still live.

At this time there was some controversy in the Jewish community, as a large number felt that the majority were no longer as orthodox as their forbears, and a conservative house of worship would be more appropriate. There were several meetings, and eventually the vote was taken and Or Shalom was affiliated to the conservative movement.

Although the majority was very happy with this change, there was a small group who were displeased, mainly immigrants who preferred to worship in the traditional style. This included my husband, who joined with a small group of men who met daily for worship in the basement of the home of Isaac Moskowitz. Although many people felt this would be a short-lived endeavor, the group grew in strength and started "Orthodox Investments" with the aim of creating a permanent home for traditional worship. Five families each invested $5,000, which was to go towards purchasing land and building a new synagogue. Needless to say, Jerry was one of the original five founders, and worked tirelessly to achieve this end. He discovered a suitable piece of property for sale at the corner of Adelaide Street and Kipps Lane and was able to acquire it at a price they could afford. There was a small house on the property, and daily services were held there.

The congregation then began the process of raising funds and eventually was able to undertake the exciting process of erecting a new synagogue. This was named the Beth Tefilah (House of Prayer) and we were able to celebrate the Jewish New Year 5726 (1966) in our new house of worship.

To Jerry this was one of the most important accomplishments of his life. He attended service daily and served as chairman of the House Committee for over 30 years. He often said that he had two homes—our home on Harrison Crescent and Beth Tefilah. Later the congregation purchased a house for the Rabbi and it became part of Jerry's responsibility to oversee this too. With my banking training I had always kept a keen eye on our household and business accounts. I noticed several minor discrepancies, which I suspected were improvements to the Rabbi's home, but when I discovered a bill for a chandelier, I was taken aback as none of our properties warranted such a lavish expense. I thought, *I must talk to Jerry about this! This has gone too far!* Then I thought again. Jerry did not play golf and had no expensive hobbies, so if he chose to spend money quietly on the synagogue, I accepted that he was entitled to do so. I never mentioned it to him.

17

Growing and Pruning

Over the years we acquired several pieces of property, including several small houses and apartments that we converted into rental units. However, I had a secret wish to own something more substantial. One day I came across a row of 18 town houses in a nice district, Arbor Glen, which was for sale. I was quite impressed by this property, and with great excitement took Jerry to see it. To my surprise, Jerry was not anxious to buy. They wanted $750,000, a tremendous sum in that day. He felt we were moving out of our league, and was worried that we could not afford such a large investment. "Such big ideas for such a small lady" he said, "How can you think of such a deal?" However, I was not to be deterred, and went to see the bank manager, Mr. Young.

He went see the property with me, then asked, "You don't have the money, Fanny?"

"No, I replied. "But I could sell 764 York Street for the down payment."

He agreed to loan me the rest of the money if I could sell the property on York Street. I was over the moon, "Thank you so much for trusting in me," I stammered. He smiled warmly. "Mrs. Goose", he said, "Successful bankers learn when to put their trust in people, not only property. I have faith in you." I felt ten feet tall, and from then on always regarded bankers as my friends.

But where would I find a buyer for the York Street property? Could I sell it in time? Within days a lawyer from the nearby city of St. Thomas contacted me on behalf of a buyer who wanted my property to build a restaurant. I asked my friend Sam Lerner, "How much should I charge him?"

Tell him $70,000," he said.

"70,000? That is too much! I am going to ask for $35,000."

"Okay," he said. "Ask him for $35,000."

I did and he paid me $35,000 in cash, which I put down on the 18 townhouses.

We settled down very comfortably in London. The boys were doing well. Martin had always been a very good and conscientious student, and we were delighted when he graduated from law school. He decided to practice in Toronto, and has excelled both professionally and in the business world.

From an early age, Steven had only one ambition: radio broadcasting. Bill Brady, a popular local radio host, was his idol. He went to Fanshawe College and graduated in media studies. Steven has become a popular radio figure, host of the morning show where he interviews local and national politicians. From time to time his program is advertised on local buses or billboards, and I am always so proud to see Steven's face adorning these ads.

Jerry and I have never really been interested in travel. That long drag across Europe at the worst possible time left us with no desire to go back, and neither of us wished to go back to Poland. We went to various parts of Canada, usually for the celebrations of friends or family. Pearl and Sam had a condominium in Miami Beach and we often took a holiday there in February, although we thought it better to stay independently at a hotel. This proved to be quite a voyage of discovery, as over the years various connections we had known from pre-war days turned up at the same hotel, which is a very popular Jewish holiday venue. Some people I had thought to have perished in the Holocaust had managed to escape and we all had stories to share of how we had survived. Of course many had the tattoo marks from the concentration camps. We have had some very pleasant holidays in Miami Beach, but I could never manage to be away for more than two weeks, as before long I always longed for home.

By the 1990's the Jewish community of London, although not large, was maintaining three synagogues and a community center as well as a Hebrew School. The idea was put forward that there was a fair amount of spare land on which the Or Shalom Synagogue and community center already stood, and it could be possible to relocate both the orthodox and reform congregations there as well, sharing certain facilities and personnel. Some people were extremely enthusiastic about the idea, but others foresaw serious difficulties. There would be great problems about kitchen facilities, for example, as there was a wide gap between the kashrus requirements of the Orthodox congregation and the wishes of the Reform members. The Beth Tefilah was very divided on the issue, with the Rabbi and younger members being for the idea and several of the older ones being adamantly opposed. Jerry was one of those opposed as he felt that our congregation had been founded to preserve the traditions that would be lost if this took place.

A meeting of the congregation was called and tempers ran very high. It was an extremely emotional meeting, and Jerry was reduced to tears and left in a very upset state. It was decided that Beth Tefilah would support the proposal.

The time of the annual general meeting was approaching, and a few days later we received the nominations list for the executive board on which Jerry had always served. To my surprise, Jerry's name, and the names of all those who had voted against the idea did not appear on the list. Knowing how upset Jerry would be, I phoned the chairman of nominations to ask whether there had been a mistake. I was told that it was time for a new look in the synagogue, and that new blood was required. I swallowed my pride, and pointed out that it meant a great deal to Jerry, and he had served for over 30 years, and wished very much to continue. The chairman told me that there was nothing further to discuss.

Of course Jerry was heartbroken, and we decided we could not remain members of a congregation, which clearly had rejected us. We returned to the Or Shalom. I must say that their congregation welcomed us with open arms, and were particularly gracious to Jerry. The president invited him to join the board immediately and to serve in any capacity he wished. Jerry had no further wish to become involved, however, although he deeply appreciated the honor of being asked. Incidentally, the proposed "merger" was turned down, and the three congregations continued separately. Within a short time the Rabbi of the Beth Tefilah had accepted another appointment and the chairman of nominations had also left town. Everything blew over, but unfortunately Jerry never recovered from it. We are still members of the Or Shalom where Jerry is regarded with great respect.

On the whole we have both been extremely fortunate with our health. We had a horrible scare some years ago when Jerry was diagnosed with a brain tumor, but fortunately it was operable and he recovered fully. We owe a lot to the skill of our local surgeons, and the wonderful hospital facilities we have in London.

I too had a bad experience in 2000. I had not been feeling well for some time and had checked with my doctor who suspected a small ulcer. I took various medications but still felt poorly and depressed. Then in April, while out for lunch with the family I collapsed and was rushed to the emergency room. They discovered internal bleeding from the ulcer, and various other complications, and operated immediately. I found myself in intensive care with tubes coming out of everywhere. I was terrified, and found all the hospital routines and treatment very scary. Due to wonderful attention I recovered, but it took a long time before I felt well again. I was very weak and depressed.

There was a good side to this experience. I was amazed to find myself surrounded by cards and flowers, and had never realized that my life had touched so many people. While I was recovering I did not feel strong enough to return to the store, so Jerry took over the daily responsibilities and I supervised the books and kept an eye on finances. Steven was wonderful. Despite having a demanding full-time job of his own, he took over the buying and looked after our rental properties. Martin, too, was a great support.

I began to feel better and returned to work. We even contemplated a holiday. Then another blow struck. Due to faulty wiring in the shop next door there was a fire, which seriously damaged several surrounding properties, including our shop and the apartment above it. It was a devastating blow. Once again I began feeling ill and was in a great deal of pain. I worried about my heart and underwent a series of tests, but nothing major emerged. Again Steven stepped in, handling insurance assessments, clearing out the smoke-damaged stock and generally preparing to reopen the shop. At that point I had no interest in continuing the business and would have been happy to close it, but Martin and Steven, very wisely, knew that Jerry would be lost without the store to manage and it was essential for his well being.

I slowly got over my malaise and began to feel more like myself. Perhaps these misfortunes served to remind us that we are only human, and that we had been very blessed. It was time to take stock and appreciate the things that had been granted to us. We had been married by this time over 50 years, and had two wonderful sons. We also had two charming and talented daughters-in-law and three splendid grandchildren. This part of our life had been very good to us.

18

Like Mother, Like Daughter

Canada had indeed been good to us, and I began to consider how I could put back something into our adopted country. Jerry had his deep and abiding interest in the synagogue, which took up much of his time and although I was involved with several local Jewish organizations, I wanted something more.

My mother had always been deeply interested in politics. Her store had been a meeting place for local politicians and for all those who had anything to say about the government. I remembered it as a vibrant, exciting place where one might find anyone from the mayor to the chief of the fire brigade or the police chief airing various ideas and listening to suggestions. Sometimes sparks flew when there was a disagreement. I had loved sneaking into a corner and listening to some of these debates. I was always proud of my mother who had plenty of ideas of her own, and frequently would hear "You know, Ettie you always hit the nail on the head. It's a shame you aren't in politics yourself." My mother would toss her head and say, "Who knows, maybe one day it might be possible!"

This all came back to me, and I began to think of taking an active interest in Canadian politics. I had always read the papers avidly as I liked to keep up to date, and was fully aware of what was going on. I thought that provincial politics would be a good area in which to start and decided to attend some meetings and find out more. The first question was to find out which party was the one for me. I had studied the ideas put forward by all the parties, and my first thought was that as a small business operator, the Conservative party seemed a natural fit, and I should try that. I learned the date of the next riding (electoral district) meeting and went along.

I should explain that at the time, the Conservative party in Ontario had held power for over 20 years. John A. Robarts, who represented my riding, was Premier, and another Londoner, John White, was Treasurer, and altogether London was quite a seat of influence.

I went to my first meeting. It was well attended, and I was not quite sure of what to do. I have to admit that I was somewhat intimidated by the gathering, and looked around for a friendly face. No one came to my rescue and I felt very much like a fish out of water. I stayed for a while and eventually went home feeling that I was not wanted in that particular party. I presumed that after so long in power, they were sufficiently established that new members were not necessary. I was disappointed, but resolved to attend the next meeting of the Liberal party I saw announced to see if I might feel more welcomed there.

Sure enough, a meeting was announced in the London Free Press and once again I made arrangements to attend. This time things were different. I was immediately introduced to various officials and my interest was very much encouraged. I had met several of the people there and was pleased when Clarence Peterson, whom I had met through business, came over to speak to me. I told him that I had earlier attended a Conservative meeting and he laughed. He told me that his original loyalty had been to the New Democratic Party, or NDP, when he lived in Saskatchewan, and that there was no harm in trying other parties first. "I predict you will end up like me – a lifelong Liberal," he said. Time has proved him right. I joined the Liberals that evening and have never changed.

I became friendly with the Peterson family. They had three sons. The oldest, Jim, was away in Ottawa, involved in the federal government, so I did not get to know him so well, and the youngest son Tim was not yet old enough to be interested in politics, but I became very close to their middle son David, who was keen to represent London in the provincial government. David encouraged my interest in politics and helped me understand complex issues, and in fact began to call me "Momma" which he still does. I have a great affection for him, his wife, Shelley and their children.

At first I was quite shy. I listened, but was not sure enough of my spoken English to express myself. I found that I could follow everything well and made mental notes of what I would have to say when I had the confidence. When I finally did speak up, I was heartened by the encouragement I received and several people supported me. People actually asked for my point of view and took notice.

At this time we did a lot of advertising on the radio. Our younger son, Steven, was always particularly interested in radio and encouraged me to listen to call-in shows, particularly the one hosted by his role model, Bill Brady. I became so interested that I began phoning the show to express my opinions. I became quite well known through this and was always surprised and delighted when other people rang in to agree or disagree with my ideas. Bill Brady was always welcoming and pleasant, and over the years he too became a great friend.

One day, much to my surprise, the then-Mayor of London, Mr. McClure, came into the store, and asked me if I would be interested in standing for the city council. I was most flattered, but felt I was not fluent enough in English, or sufficiently aware of the issues to be of use. He told me that he had heard me on the radio shows, and was very impressed by my grip on local issues. "We need you, Mrs. Goose," he told me. "We have been very self-centered Londoners for a long time. Now we are getting a lot of new citizens from all over the world, and we have to learn what they are thinking and get a new perspective." I told him that I was very honored by his kind opinion, but l was too involved with running my business to do a good job. He told me not to give up my interest as I had a lot to offer.

My elder son, Martin, was also fascinated by politics, and was an officer in the University Liberal Club. Pierre Trudeau came to speak to the students, and of course I went to hear him. Martin introduced me, and I found him very charming. Some time later he came to London again, this time to speak in the public square behind the city hall. I was surprised and flattered when he noticed me in the crowd, remembered my name and invited me to join him on the platform. I was always greatly impressed by Mr. Trudeau's memory. Despite all the people he met everywhere, he always greeted me by name when we would meet at Liberal party conventions.

I thoroughly enjoyed the Liberal party meetings and met many interesting people. I helped with the fund raising, and even went door-to-door with candidates at election time. As Mayor McClure had predicted, more and more immigrants were coming to Ontario, including London, and my accent was becoming an asset, showing that politics was open to all. Times were changing, and governments could change too.

19

Friends From the Past

One afternoon I was working in the shop as usual when a woman came in. She looked vaguely familiar, but I had a lot of regular customers and did not think too much about it. Then I heard the door, and Martin returning from school. "Is that you Zenya?" I called. Zenya was still our nickname for Martin. The woman started, came nearer and looked at me closely. "Goose, Gusz?" she began slowly. "I did not connect it. Could you possibly be Fanie Gusz?" She had a Polish accent so I realized we had perhaps met elsewhere, but still could not place her exactly. "Do you not remember me?" she asked, "I am Janet, who looked after Zenya on the trip from Hamburg."

Memories of that terrible trip came flooding back. Jerry and I had been so ill, and this wonderful girl had taken complete charge of our lively son, who did not know the meaning of seasickness. "Of course," I gasped, "How could I forget you?" "I am not surprised you put that trip out of your mind," she replied. "You and Jerry were both so horribly ill."

"How wonderful to see you," I replied sincerely, "But what are you doing here? I thought you were on your way somewhere else."

"I live here now," Janet told me. "I stayed in Quebec for a while, then met my husband. He was offered a job here, so we came to London. I am Janet Kosemba now. But you were going to Toronto and I never expected you to be here. A friend recommended your shop, and I came in to pick up some things for my children."

We of course lapsed into Polish, and arranged to meet to share more about our lives in Canada. I was delighted to see her, as she was a lively intelligent woman, and we became close friends. I met her husband and discovered that both of them were in jobs not worthy of their skills, and I determined to help them find something better. Janet's sister-in-law, Donna, was also a bright, ambitious girl, so I suggested that the two of them open a dress shop. They loved the idea, and I was able to help them find a suitable property and obtain loans as well as give them general advice. I introduced Janet's husband to a friend of mine in real estate, and when he discovered he had a flair for selling properties, they set up a successful partnership. I was thrilled to be able to help them in this way.

Janet introduced me to Pauline Kostuik, another Polish success story. She had come over with her family to start a new life in Canada as they had so little opportunity in Poland. Not being Jewish, they had not faced the persecution that we had, but conditions in Poland were very hard and they wanted to start a life with more opportunity. The family had all done very well, and when I met her she was extremely wealthy. She had married another Polish immigrant, and they had property all over the world. She loved clothes, and dressed extravagantly. She had a collection of shoes that rivaled that of Imelda Marcos. I once teased her about her enormous variety of shoes, and she told me that the first winter they were in Canada her mother had told her and her sister that they could only afford to have one pair of shoes each. Her mother had decided that black rubber Wellington boots would be best, as they would be suitable for bad weather and could be lined with socks to be warm. They could also be cleaned up and shined to wear with dresses. Pauline told me that by the end of that winter her feet were sore and she hated the boots. She then promised herself that one day she would have shoes to match every outfit. I never teased her again about her shoes.

Among many investments all over the world, Pauline owned the two high-rise blocks of apartments that faced our row of town-houses on Arbour Glen, so we had shared interests there. She was extremely philanthropic, supporting many charities. She loved music and was very involved with the Chopin competition in Warsaw, which she always attended. She was also very supportive of the Catholic University of Lublin in Poland, and raised funds avidly. One of her major fundraisers for them was an annual garden party, which I always attended. It was a wonderful excuse each year to buy a new hat—my weakness!

We became good friends. Pauline always supported my charities and I hers. She made a most generous donation to the synagogue when I was collecting for a new roof. I helped her raise money and contributed to the Catholic University. It was interesting that, although I did not know it until much later, the Lublin University had steadfastly maintained its Department of Jewish Studies right through the Russian occupation—the only one of its kind in Poland.

Pauline invited me to her home one day to meet an important Polish friend, the Archbishop of Krakow, who was her houseguest. I remember this very well. It was a beautiful day, and we sat by Pauline's pool. He had been in Poland through the German occupation, and had practiced his faith in secret. We talked over those terrible days, and he told me he had been able to save many Jewish lives. I told him that the Catholic priests had provided me with sanctuary too and we both felt this was a bond between us. He was a remarkable man and exuded the presence of God. I was not surprised when he later became Pope—Pope John Paul II. Pauline had several audiences with him, and told me that he always asked after "Franciska" as he called me.

Pauline was a staunch Catholic, and very involved with the church. Most of the Polish immigrants came immediately to the church, and Father Peter suggested that Pauline and I might be able to offer them advice and possibly assistance in a new country. I was only too willing to help and found my contacts very useful in finding them jobs—or just giving advice on where to go for help. I began to understand the meaning of the North American term "networking". Of course this soon developed from merely Polish immigrants to any nationality and I was always happy to do what I could. Coming into our store was easier and less intimidating than having to meet with government officials and I loved being able to help make the transition to Canadian life easier for those who sought my counsel.

That was how my involvement with "New Canadians" began, and to this day, people drop in to my store to ask advice on "settling in" here. I take this responsibility very seriously.

20

Eretz Israel

I had never been particularly orthodox in my religion, but my grandfather had taken care to see that he instill in me as much faith as possible, along with respect for our Jewish traditions. Jerry is strictly observant and derives great joy from his observance, but I am rather more casual. However, I took a great interest in the synagogue and its daily administration. I love fundraising and organization and served on the Sisterhood—the equivalent of a Women's Guild—in every position from president downwards.

Strangely, although as a child I had always been a tomboy, in adulthood I developed a passion for dolls, and have a houseful full of them. Every time there was a celebration or party, I would appear with another gorgeous doll to raffle for whatever cause we were supporting. Over the years I made quite a lot of money for charity from my doll collection. I have also been involved in Hadassah, our women's organization that supports many projects in Israel. Every year I would take an active part in our annual bazaar, which is a major fundraiser. As always, when I do anything I throw myself into it heart and soul, and over the years have had great fun working with the Hadassah women to raise money for worthy causes.

In all my years here, I have made only one journey outside North America. This was my unforgettable trip to Israel. Despite what I have said about not being overly religious, I was deeply moved by this experience. In 1973 the Rabbi of the Or Shalom organized a trip from London and I decided to go. Jerry stayed home, literally to mind the shop, and I went on my own with the group from the synagogue.

It was a very long flight and we were all quite exhausted when we arrived. However, there is something about being in Israel that revives one instantly, and I stood there, hardly believing that I was actually in the land of the Bible. The whole time I was there I seemed to feel my grandfather's presence. He had spoken so often and so lovingly of "Eretz Israel," and I felt that I was tremendously privileged to be in the land of which he could only dream. I have to say that I felt rather unworthy—*why should I have been the fortunate one to have this experience when so many had been denied it?*

We did a great deal of sightseeing, of course, and it was a wonderful experience seeing those places that had been only biblical names to me. When I saw a dog one day, I amused all my companions by saying that even the dog was Jewish and when I discovered that his name was *Shalom*, meaning "Peace," it seemed very fitting. At that time Jerusalem was still divided and we could not see all of the Old City, but we were still feeling somewhat overcome at just being there.

I had a most interesting experience in Jerusalem. I met a lady whom I had previously known years ago in Skalat. She had survived the Holocaust and had come to Israel and married a lawyer called Weizman. It was wonderful to know that someone else from our little town had escaped and I was very happy to see her. The next day I was sitting in the lounge of the King David hotel, when I heard the name "Fanie Steinbock" being called out. I was rather surprised as I had not carried that name for many years, but I went to the desk to inquire if it was for me. There was a very good-looking man in military uniform waiting for me. "I do apologize for using your maiden name," he said, "But when Mrs. Weizman told me she had seen you, she told me that you had been so busy reminiscing that she forgot to ask your married name." We both laughed, and I told him I was now Fanny Goose, and he told me he was Jannick Landsberg.

The past all came flooding back. There had been a glorious summer and my aunt's younger sister had come to visit. This was very exciting as she was a quite a celebrity, a former Miss Poland, and a beautiful girl. I was quite awed. Her name was Rachella Polichuk and of course she immediately attracted the attention of all the young men for miles around, and our home was busier than ever. Jannick, who came from a very wealthy family, was the favored suitor. This delighted me, as Jannick had the smartest car in town— an open sports car—and was good-natured enough to take me for rides, usually when he was waiting for Rachella. It had come to nothing, as Rachella had met a handsome army officer in dazzling uniform and her fancy had changed.

I remember one encounter between my grandfather and the glamorous officer, who was not Jewish. My grandfather was leaving the house for the synagogue on a *Shabbat* morning. The officer in all his glory—Polish army uniforms were very ornate—and my grandfather in his prayer shawl and yarmulke stared at each other, looking as if each were from another world. I thought it was terribly funny at the time!

I believe Rachella subsequently married a Russian, but after her marriage I never heard of her again. Until this moment, I had completely forgotten her, but it was wonderful to remember this happy time and to meet with someone from the distant past and learn that they too had survived.

The whole trip to Israel was a revelation. Not merely seeing the ancient sites, but the modern miracles that had been wrought there. I was particularly fascinated by the way the agricultural experts had been able to turn the desert into fertile land. That awakened my interest in the JNF, the Jewish National Fund, a charitable organization that plants trees in Israel, and I became an active member and supporter of this organization. In 2004 Jerry and I were chosen as honorees for the Negev dinner, JNF's major fundraising event. We deeply appreciated this. Our only condition was that the project designated to be constructed in our name should be something beneficial to all Israelis regardless of religion or ethnic background.

JNF proposed the establishment of a recreation area at Shomera, one kilometer from the Lebanese border. There were no facilities there and the plan was to create a restful and serene atmosphere for people to visit, also preserving a grove of indigenous trees. We were delighted with this idea. The dinner was a tremendous success, and we were touched by the large attendance. So many people from Toronto wished to attend that Martin decided to arrange a bus to convey them to London and back. It was a memorable event and we were very proud. The JNF was also the beneficiary when in 2000 the Scotia Bank asked us to choose a recipient for a large donation they made in our name.

I have also been enormously impressed by the work and research that is carried out in Israel for children and became involved in a program to bring Jewish young people to Israel, called Youth Aliyah. Through this I gained the title *Ima*, "Mother in Israel." Jerry and I are also proud recipients of the Ben Gurion award, for our part in selling Israeli bonds.

In 2005 the London Friends of Canadian Magen David Adom (the equivalent of the Red Cross) decided to raise funds to provide a fully equipped and Canadian-made ambulance to Israel from the London Jewish community. We all supported the project whole-heartedly and I was deeply honored when, funds having been raised, I was invited to cut the ribbon at the dedication of the ambulance. I did so with great pride and a fervent prayer that the ambulance be used to save lives in peacetime rather than for victims of hostilities.

Altogether my one-time trip to Israel was deeply moving and very thrilling. Despite the hard conditions of daily life, the Israelis seemed to follow an old motto my grandfather used to recite: "Work as if you will live forever, but live as if every day is your last!" It was the liveliest possible place in the evenings. The cafes were full and noisy, as Israelis are not a quiet people, and the atmosphere was tremendous. I loved going out in the evenings and on one occasion I got locked out of the hotel. Security was tight and when my friends and I arrived back, none of us could remember the password of the day. The porter told us that he could not let us in, and we had to wait outside until someone finally came along to identify us.

While I had a wonderful time in Israel and loved the country and deeply respect the people for their incredible achievements, I was still glad to return to my Canadian home. To me, being safe in my own home is the best thing in the world.

I do not like to travel far from home, but when I was in my seventies, we went to Nassau where we met a beautiful Austrian woman, perhaps five years younger than I, who was staying in the next room in our hotel. Nassau is quite popular with German tourists, and we have enjoyed meeting other guests in the past, but this particular woman was at my side everywhere I went—swimming in the pool, on shopping trips and all throughout the evening of cocktails, dinner, and dancing. She even unpacked my bags for me when I first arrived. I thought this was very strange, so I asked her why she was so devoted to me.

"I want to ask you one thing," she said.

"Go ahead and ask," I said. "If I know the answer, I will tell you."

"I heard you are Jewish and I have a question for you. What does it mean when you go like this," she made circles with both hands meeting in the middle, palms down, "over candles."

"Ah!" I said. "It is a Jewish tradition, a blessing. You can have two candles or five candles, and you go like this," I motioned with my hands, "on Friday night, to bless the home as the Sabbath begins. Why does this concern you?"

"I remember this!" she said with great enthusiasm, as if I had solved a great mystery. "I can see it in my mind. I can never get this picture out of my mind. Someone is doing this, but I don't know where the memory comes from."

Two days later, I was leaving. She was staying a month there, while my vacation had been only two weeks. We had gotten to be very close, so she came over to pack my bags for me.

"Let it be," I urged her. "You are happy now, why does it matter?"

She bit her lip and said, "I can't let it go. It bothers me. I have already called my mother in Austria and told her what you said about the candles. She said that she would tell me about it when I got home."

A few weeks later I got a letter from her. Her father had been an Austrian officer in the German army during the war. He apparently found her, a precious little girl with blond curls sleeping on the steps in Warsaw, just four years old. He took her into his arms and arranged for her to be sent to his wife in Austria. The father never came back from the war, but the mother raised her. She was undoubtedly a Jewish child whose family had been killed.

It was hard to remember that eerie, difficult time when some lived and others died through the strangest of circumstances.

21

Politics and More Politics

I remained very involved with the Liberal party. To me it was an outlet. I loved the meetings, thoroughly enjoying meeting new and interesting people and immersing myself in the excitement of political conventions. In Ontario things had been pretty static for some time; the Tories had been in power provincially for what seemed like forever, while the Trudeau years had been solidly Liberal at the federal level.

However, in the 1970s there was a feeling of change in the air and people began to think that the Tory stranglehold on Ontario could be broken. The most exciting thing to me was that my dear friend David Peterson was elected as a Member of Provincial Parliament for London North in 1975. David's election went against the tide of public opinion nationally, as the election was a terrible defeat for the Liberals, who finished in third place behind the NDP. But it was a huge boost for us in London North. I had gone door-to-door with David, and worked very hard, and felt euphoric about his win.

The poor result for the party naturally led to a leadership convention, and somewhat to our surprise David, although a rather new member, made a bid for the job. He was defeated by Stuart Smith, an eloquent member from Hamilton, but would live to fight another day. The Tories remained in power, but after Bill Davies retired there were divisions in the party and we began to think that a breakthrough was imminent. Stuart Smith resigned and there was another leadership convention in 1981.

I remember that convention vividly as it was so exciting. David stood again, and I was very active in soliciting votes and doing all I could to support him. It was even better when the results were announced and my dear friend was elected leader. I was so excited, and of course there were some great celebrations. One of the wonderful things about political conventions is that no matter what, there is an optimistic spirit and great parties! I thoroughly enjoyed myself.

In 1985 another Londoner, Don Smith, was elected leader of the Ontario Liberal party and we really began to think that London was becoming the hub of the party. In 1985 there was provincial election that the Liberals won. I could hardly believe it, *"Just think,"* I said to myself, *The premier of Ontario calls me "Momma!"* David insisted I come to his swearing in and even offered to take me in the helicopter but I settled for more conventional transport.

Those were very heady years. My downtown store became the center I had always dreamed about. All sorts of people used it as a meeting place as it was very convenient, just like my mother's store. If you dropped into Goose's Family Clothing you might see anyone there, from the premier on down.

I went several times to meetings in Toronto and have many wonderful memories from these trips. One evening after a rather busy meeting we went out to dine in a group. Everyone relaxed over wine and ordered exotic dishes. I was quite unsure about the menu, and decided to play it safe by ordering fish and chips!

Another time we were chatting after some business, and David said, "Come along Momma. I'll take you home now." I was having a really good time, and wasn't at all tired, so I said, "No, David, you go along and I will get a lift back." Everybody laughed, and I was teased for a long time about refusing a ride with the premier of Ontario.

The Liberal hold on the provincial government was tenuous at that time as it was formed through an alliance with the New Democratic Party, neither party having won a majority of the seats in the legislature. When the time seemed right, David called another election that we won with a majority. Things seemed to be going very well and he decided to call another election in the hope of increasing the majority to have an even stronger mandate from the public. I had an odd feeling about this and advised David not to call it despite the press polls showing good support for him and the party. Of course mine was only a hunch and the wise pundits advised otherwise, but alas, we lost the election to the NDP. Even David lost his seat. It was a tremendously sad day.

The NDP under their leader Bob Rae took over and then in the election following the Tories were thrust back into power. Our member was Dianne Cunningham, and despite the difference in our parties, we had many of the same views regarding London, and she was very supportive of my ideas.

Federally there were big changes too. Trudeau had been Prime Minister since 1968, with the exception of a brief period in 1979-80 when the Conservatives won the election and Trudeau had resigned. However, before a new Liberal leader could be elected, Prime Minister Joe Clark called another election and Trudeau reversed his decision and stayed on to lead the Liberals into that election, which we won. Trudeau finally resigned in 1984.

At the leadership convention to find a replacement for Trudeau, I was jubilant because the candidate I supported, John Turner, won. Everyone teased me because John Turner was a very handsome man, and I was accused of supporting him for his lovely blue eyes. I had met him several times and had a great admiration for him. I thought he was very competent. Sadly, he lost the election and has the dubious distinction of being Canada's shortest reigning Prime Minister.

The next and last time I attended a convention was in Calgary in 1990. I was supporting Paul Martin, a man I knew and admired. The convention, however, voted overwhelmingly for Jean Chretien, so I was not as happy. I saw Pierre Trudeau at the convention, but he merely nodded to me this time. I think it was because I was decked out with Paul Martin buttons and he had thrown his support behind Chretien.

I have always maintained my interest in politics, but am no longer so active. Joe Fontana, who was the Member of Parliament in London North Center for 18 years, was a good friend and often dropped into the store to talk to me. Before he stood for parliament Joe had served as a city alderman—a very young one. At one point he considered running for mayor, and came into the store to discuss it with me. I advised him against it—I thought he was too young and besides I suspected he had other ambitions.

I supported Joe strongly when he became our local riding candidate and later federal member, but did not approve of his decision to resign and cause a federal by-election in the fall of 2006, as I thought it endangered the seat. However, Glen Pearson retained it for the Liberals. I was very interested to meet Elizabeth May, the leader of the Green Party, who ran in the by-election and called into the store to meet me.

My friend, Dianne Haskett, the former mayor of London (1994–2000), suffered a devastating loss as the Conservative nominee in that same election. She had moved six years earlier with her family to the U.S. and her return to run for the seat was seen as opportunistic by the public even though she had been a popular mayor. I knew Dianne well enough to know that she did not return out of political ambition but only out of a desire to serve and I tried to encourage her during the months that followed as she recovered from the sense of rejection she felt from her loss.

22

"First Lady of Downtown"

I have always been a firm believer that the downtown is the heart and core of a city, and as such, it should be flourishing and vital. Maybe it is my European upbringing, my age or perhaps the fact that I don't drive, but I do not like shopping malls. I feel that they are characterless collections of shops, and in no way add to the city character. To me, there is nothing like walking down the main street to judge the personality of the city. I was thrilled to be becoming part of this.

This sentiment has never left me. I have fought long and hard to help revitalize and recreate a vibrant downtown and I regard these efforts as among my most important endeavors. I became an active member of the London Downtown Business Association and served on its Board of Directors for many years. In 2000, Fred Kingsmill and I were made the first appointees to an Honorary Advisory Board.

I was extremely fortunate in having Fred Kingsmill as my neighbor. Despite my initial misgivings and the enormous disparity between us, Fred and I have shared the same viewpoint on most issues and have worked together very effectively. We really represent the full gamut. The Kingsmills are old Londoners, whereas we are first generation immigrants; Fred's elegant well-established emporium is a far cry from our higgledy-piggledy family store. He is a Conservative and I am a Liberal. Even though we see eye-to-eye on most things, it has to be sitting down as he is a good foot taller than I. We have fought many battles together for the city, and I hope we will continue to do so for many years.

In 1998 Jerry and I received the Police Certificate of Appreciation for our work with "Crimebusters." I always smile when I look at this certificate. I was asked by the police to participate in a novel scheme. They would publicly "imprison" leading citizens, and demand a ransom to release them. This was a lot of fun, and I was "held" behind bars in the middle of Galleria Mall. Jerry arrived, and asked the police how much it would take to ensure I was NOT released. Fortunately many of my friends arrived and paid the "ransom," and despite his unsuccessful attempt to keep me behind bars, Jerry also gave generously.

I look upon my unofficial work for the city as my most important contribution. I tried whenever possible to use the connections I made through my political involvement to assist in getting support for many projects which have benefited London. I was invited to sit on the committee choosing recipients for the Order of Canada, but declined as I could not attend all the necessary meetings in Ottawa and besides I did not think I was qualified to judge such notable people in so many different fields outside my locale and experience. I did propose Bill Brady, however, for this honor. He has been a wonderful community worker for London, tirelessly giving his time and expertise to so many different causes. I was delighted when it was awarded to him. He amused many people when he was once asked to characterize me. He described me as "a modern day, Kosher Mother Theresa." Not quite true, but I was very flattered.

I did, however, agree to become a member of the National Heritage Commission, as this was a wonderful platform for helping London. I was able to put forward London projects for funding and was successful in many cases. This position generated a constant stream of would-be recipients pleading their case for extra funding. I listened carefully to them all and I hope I made wise decisions as to which causes to promote.

Jerry and I tried to accommodate and promote as many different causes as we could, from Theatre London and the Art Gallery to Women's Community House and the Ronald McDonald House. For a time, I served on the board of Orchestra London. Health issues have always mattered to me a great deal, and we have always been major supporters of the various hospitals as well as the cancer association, heart and stroke fund and many more. We support the St Josephs Hospital Foundation strongly—and not only because our daughter-in-law is president of the foundation, and vice president of fund raising.

Several of our city's mayors have sought advice from me, and many would-be city councilors have asked for my opinion. I certainly do not think I am infallible, but probably representative of the average Londoner. I can only offer common sense and a lot of experience in understanding people.

As part of my desire to see downtown revitalized, I strongly supported the City in its efforts to acquire a large block of land at the western end of downtown for the construction of a sports and entertainment center.

Once a deal was arranged for the land to be purchased, the fun began. Virtually everyone had a different idea about how to use the land. London had for a long time been lamenting the lack of an arena or a performing arts center, and I saw the opportunity to remedy that lack right here, and bring new life to downtown.

There was a lively debate. A vocal group objected to the destruction of the Talbot Inn, a heritage building still standing on the site, but the parcel on which the inn sat would be necessary if we were to have enough land to build an arena. The idea of preserving the façade of the inn as part of the development seemed acceptable to most, and I set up a petition in my store asking that the land be used as an arena. I also contacted other storekeepers and encouraged them to support it—and get more signatures on the petition. I alone obtained well over 2,000 signatures. On June 3rd 2001, with no further ado, the city began construction of the new John Labatt Center, which would become a focal point for our community.

Of course there were further arguments. I favored using local contractors for the job, particularly when we had a good firm like Ellis-Don in the city. Some people had different ideas, but in the end the contract went to Ellis-Don.

Because I was apparently seen as a prime mover for this project and often referred to as "the First Lady of Downtown", I was invited to participate in the public ground breaking ceremony with the mayor and a city controller. Afterwards I was presented with the shovel I had used and I am very proud of that souvenir.

The rest is history. The Labatt company donated a large sum of money in order to have the facility designated the John Labatt Center and a magnificent building was erected and was opened in October 2002. Now London has a state-of-the-art venue for performance events which seats over 10,000 and can seat 9,000 for hockey and ice events. It hosts everything from Broadway shows to operas, Cirque du Soleil, Disney on Ice, and top international performers such as Elton John, Cher, Julie Andrews, Shania Twain, Bob Dylan, Rod Stewart and B.B. King. Even President Bill Clinton has spoken there!

I was invited to the gala opening and for the first and probably last time in my life, I danced on the stage. Another first for me is that I appear in the foreground of a photograph from the opening ceremony that hangs in the sports bar. To my knowledge it is the only photograph of me displayed in a bar!

The center is now home to the London Knights hockey team, which previously used the outdated Ice House, far from the center of London. The Knights hosted the 2005 Memorial Cup—which they won—as well as the Ontario Hockey League Championship.

2004-2005 was a spectacularly successful season for them, and generated great excitement throughout the city. Half the local cars flew Knights pennants and hockey fever was the order of the day. When they won the Cup, I felt as if I had scored the winning goal myself.

As I had hoped, the arena has rejuvenated this part of downtown. There are now many new restaurants and businesses in this area and people flow through. It is wonderful to see all of our efforts to create a stronger core in the center of our city bearing such fruit.

23

Blossoming

I have worked closely with many of London's mayors: Al Gleeson, Tom Gosnell, Dianne Haskett and current Mayor Anne Marie DeCicco-Best. Regardless of political affiliation we have all worked together well, and I am happy to count them all among my personal friends.

I was privileged to attend the lighting of the Eternal Flame at Frederick Banting House when Her Majesty the Queen Mother visited London for this purpose in 1989. The museum honors the discoverer of insulin and the flame is to remain lit until a permanent cure is found for diabetes. The lighting was followed by a very pleasant luncheon at the Art Gallery. I was seated quite near Her Majesty and saw how beautifully she put everyone at ease. It was an arduous schedule for a woman in her 90th year and we all admired her stamina and grace.

Another notable royal occasion was when Her Majesty the Queen visited London in June 1997. It was a beautiful day, and Harris Park made a perfect setting. We were sitting in rows as Her Majesty came by and she gave me quite a long look. My neighbor murmured, "Her Majesty must like you, Fanny," but I shook my head. "No way", I said, "I know that look. She is admiring my hat." I had purchased a very special hat for this occasion, beige organdy piled high with flowers made from the same fabric as the hat, and personally felt that it deserved notice!

The Canadian Heritage Commission appointed me to the "Celebrate Canada Day" committee for Ontario. I loved this job, and dreamed up various projects to add to the excitement. My friend and downtown neighbor, Pat Georgeopoulus and I organized a pancake breakfast on Dundas Street hosted by the retailers of the street. With my lack of culinary expertise, I left the pancakes to the expert Pat, and busied myself serving and handing out goodies. It was a great success. I always love to see Dundas Street full of people.

I have derived enormous joy from participating in the Canada Day celebrations through the years. I particularly remember 1997 when there was a very large crowd, and as a member of the national Heritage Commission, I was officiating. The central feature was the swearing in of new Canadian citizens, and it was my pleasure to welcome them.

I decided to borrow from the famous words of John F. Kennedy, words which have always moved me. I said how pleased we were that so many people had decided to make Canada their home and trusted that they would find much happiness as Canadians. "But don't expect everything for nothing," I told them. "Citizenship carries responsibility as well. Don't ask what Canada can do for you; ask what you can do for Canada." Several people afterwards remarked that I had used the words of John Kennedy, but I felt it was the right thing to say. That speech rang very true—it is the way I have always tried to act and I wanted to impress on all these new Canadians that they too should think like this.

In 2005 the London Free Press published a list of the 150 people, past and present, who "defined London." I was very happy to be featured amongst them, with the appellation "Godmother of Downtown." It was a very gratifying tribute. And I was extremely honored when the Downtown Business Association commissioned a portrait of me that was subsequently hung in their window after it was presented in a special ceremony.

Another memorable event for me was my 80th birthday. Unknown to me, my family had arranged a surprise birthday party at the London Club. I was quite amazed by the huge number of people who came to wish me well. Joe Fontana brought greetings from the government and presented me with the Queen's Jubilee medal. This was an honor I deeply appreciated. Looking round at the sea of faces, I was astonished to see how many civic leaders and very busy people had found time to join us for this special day. I felt very grateful for my happy and rewarding years in London.

24

Bearing Fruit —
The Miracle of Survival

W e are now well into the first decade of the 21st century and as I look back over my life, I am amazed at how far we have come. Jerry and I still live in London, Ontario, and have no intention of ever leaving. This is our home.

I still maintain the store with Steven's invaluable assistance, but I am getting tired. Yet I do not want to give up my central "hub." I love being where people drop in at all times and where I get all the up-to-date news. But the retail business is becoming too much for me. I am thinking of leasing the front part of my shop and just keeping an office for myself in the rear. We will see what the future brings. I would find it very hard to leave my much loved downtown.

We are enormously proud of our family. Martin is a successful lawyer and developer in Toronto. His wife, Heather, is an employ-ment counselor and they are both very active in community work. Their three children are all university graduates. Danielle has fol-lowed in Martin's footsteps, and is practicing law with a Toronto firm. She was recently married. Michael has his business degree from Dalhousie University and is working in New York City, as is his sister, Rebecca, who also graduated from Dalhousie and is now a teacher.

Steven continues his successful career in broadcasting, and is a well-known local figure. His early admiration for Bill Brady has never wavered, and Bill is now a very close family friend. Steven's wife, Michelle, is president of the St. Josephs Health Care Foundation and vice president of Fund Development. She keeps me in close touch with all that is going on, and I support the foundation fervently.

I love Christmas. Even though we do not celebrate it as a religious festival, I love the decorations, gifts, and paraphernalia surrounding it. As soon as the season approaches, I am in Kingsmill's china department admiring the wares, like a horse champing at the bit. I love all the whimsical figurines, and teapots with Father Christmas on them, and all the rest of the imaginative novelties. I spend hours devising the right present for the right person, and always arrange to have them as extravagantly wrapped as possible. I only hope the recipients enjoy receiving their gifts as much as I enjoy selecting them.

On Jerry's 80th birthday, our children honored us by donating a new dining room in our name to Baycrest, a Toronto health science center focused on aging. Then, on the occasion of our golden wedding, they had a library of Judaica dedicated to us in the Chabad Lubavitch Center at Thornhill, about 15 miles north of Toronto. We found it very gratifying that our children should choose to recognize us in this way. Jerry and I have always been strong believers in philanthropy; this was something we learned from our parents and we have always felt it important to support good causes as much as possible, and it was wonderful to see our children following the principles we hold dear. As always on such occasions, I thought of my own parents and deeply regretted that they had been deprived of experiencing such joyous occasions.

In August of this year, the London Press Club is honoring my friend Fred Kingsmill and me for our years of service to the community. My son, Steven, will serve as master-of-ceremony.

It has been a rather unsettling experience looking back across my life for the writing of this book. While many of these stories have brought back good memories, it is impossible to remember those terrible war years without intense emotion. I always wondered, *Why me? Why did I survive when so many good people died horrible deaths?* I had a most wonderful childhood, and was nurtured in the love of my parents and grandparents. I feel that somehow all this love wove a cocoon of protection around me.

When I think of the miracles that happened to ensure my safety I have to believe that God was looking after me. I nearly boarded a cattle car to Treblinka, but was dragged out of the line by a complete stranger, an Italian soldier who had no reason to care for me. The Bohannic home where I was sheltered was the only house in the village left standing, and the railway master walked me out of the *lager* just moments before the remaining Jews were gunned down. Again and again, people risked their lives to warn me, to hide me, and to provide for me. There is no explanation except to acknowledge that a divine power was protecting me. Yet I do not understand why my life was miraculously spared when for so many others, life was snatched away.

I have never returned to Poland. I have no desire to go. Sometimes I wonder what happened to Castle Zadniesowka, but I am quite certain the Nazis destroyed it as they razed all the homes owned by Jews. I have never inquired nor do I really want to know. That early part of my life holds wonderful memories but seems almost unreal to me now.

I think of the many times during my life when I recalled the voice of my grandfather. During my trip to Israel I felt his memory very strongly and I often remembered his words of wisdom during various crises in my life. My grandfather had modeled to me how important it was to nurture good relationships in the community and it may have been this that saved me during the war. There were many people who could have betrayed me at various times, but everyone, regardless of race or creed, protected me at great personal risk. For this I am enormously grateful.

Why was I chosen to be a survivor? Why was the tree that my father planted to commemorate the day of my birth the only thing still standing after all around it was destroyed? I wonder if in the future a descendant of mine might possibly do great things for mankind? In the meantime, I am simply grateful for all of God's blessings and for the fruit that has been borne in my life; I cherish my family, my friends, and my community. I have loved being able to play a supportive role in the life of my city, and hope that I have made a difference. I have done my best.